SHORT WALKS

Cambridgeshire Pubs

Jean and Geoff Pratt

COUNTRYSIDE BOOKS
NEWBURY, BERKSHIRE

COUNTRYSIDE BOOKS
3 Catherine Road
Newbury, Berkshire

ISBN 1 85306 394 0

Designed by Mon Mohan
Cover illustration by Colin Doggett
Photographs and maps by the authors

Produced through MRM Associates Ltd., Reading
Typeset by The Midlands Book Typesetting Company, Loughborough
Printed by Woolnough Bookbinding, Irthlingborough

Contents

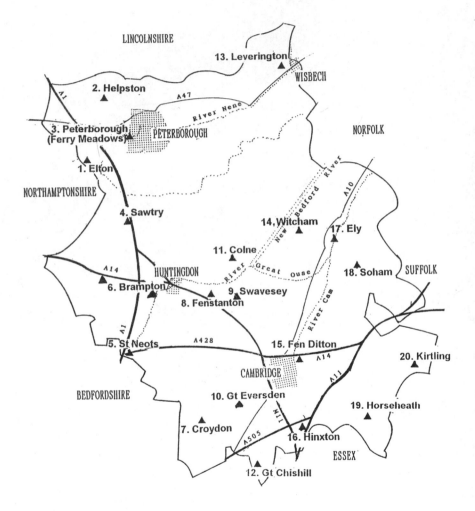

Map showing the locations of the walks.

Publisher's Note

We hope that you obtain considerable enjoyment from this book; great care has been taken in its preparation. However, changes of landlord and actual closures are sadly not uncommon. Likewise, although at the time of publication all routes followed public rights of way or permitted paths, diversion orders can be made and permissions withdrawn.

We cannot of course be held responsible for such diversion orders and any inaccuracies in the text which result from these or any other changes to the routes nor any damage which might result from walkers trespassing on private property. However, we are anxious that all details covering the walks and the pubs are kept up to date and would therefore welcome information from readers which would be relevant to future editions.

Introduction

Cambridgeshire is an agricultural county, but 300 years ago a large part of it was an extensive tract of inhospitable marshy bog surrounding an island of higher land called the Isle of Ely, on which St Etheldreda had founded an abbey in AD 673. The action of a number of enterprising men in causing the fens to be drained brought about a gradual, but far-reaching change in both the landscape and the economics of the area, which is now fertile and profitable farmland producing a variety of food crops. A criss-cross network of watercourses discharge to the rivers, which have themselves been straightened, bypassed and controlled.

The variety of the Cambridgeshire landscape can be experienced on these 20 short walks in different parts of the county. One route passes Ely Cathedral, another follows part of a Roman road, and yet another is through a country park just 3 miles from Peterborough city centre. All the walks are either along public rights of way shown on the definitive map, or on paths through public parks. They are, without exception, easily tackled and should be suitable for all ages.

The condition of footpaths and bridleways underfoot, and the degree of hindrance from vegetation, can change very quickly depending upon the weather, the amount of use and the season of the year. It is always advisable, therefore, to have stout footwear.

The sketch maps should be sufficient for route finding, but are not to scale. Although some hedges, fences, gates and so on are shown, they are there as landmarks and not all such details are indicated. Many of you may also like to carry an Ordnance Survey map and so the number of the relevant Landranger sheet is given with each walk.

In the route descriptions:

A cross-hedge, fence or ditch, is a field boundary at right angles to the direction of the walk.

A culvert is a crossing of a ditch where the ditch has been piped, and the pipe then covered with soil and stones.

A dog-leg is a turn to the left followed shortly by a turn to the right, and vice versa.

A green lane is a track or footpath hedged on both sides.

A headland is the strip of uncultivated land along the edge of a field, adjacent to a hedge, fence or ditch. Hence a headland path is a footpath along the headland.

A cross-field path is one that is not along the headland.

Do please remember to follow the country code, shut all gates and keep dogs on leads.

Each walk starts and ends at a pub selected for its welcome, its enjoyable food, its attractive appearance and, of course, the potential for a pleasant ramble in the vicinity. All of the pubs chosen welcome family groups and many have play apparatus for young children.

Opening times vary from pub to pub. However, the majority of those mentioned in this book are open between 11.30 am and 2.30 pm and again between 6.30 pm and 11 pm on Monday to Saturday. On Sunday most are open from 12 noon to 3 pm and 7 pm to 10.30 pm. Food is usually served from 12 noon to 2.30 pm and 6.30 pm to 9.30 pm. Any significant difference, by more than 30 minutes either way, is referred to in the text. A variety of bar snacks is usually available as an alternative to the menus described.

Most pubs have their own adequate car park for customers. If you intend to leave a car in the grounds whilst following a walk, it is reasonable and courteous always to ask the landlord's permission first. Parking elsewhere than in a recognised car park can be difficult. Remember that modern large farm equipment travels from farm to farm, so if you park along a country road, always ensure that an absolutely enormous tractor could get past!

We are grateful for the help given by members of the County Council's staff in the Rural Group, who know all about the rights of way in the county. Our thanks also to Mr Bradley of the Nene Park Trust, who has given helpful advice.

It is our hope that readers will derive as much pleasure from these walks and these pubs as we have done.

Jean and Geoff Pratt
Spring 1996

1 Elton
The Black Horse

At the edge of Cambridgeshire, on the east bank of the river Nene, stands the small and attractive village of Elton, with quiet streets flanked by many cottages of warm, cream stone. Nearby, in summer, children splash in a sandy backwater while holiday barges sail the river, en route to negotiate the lock beside the old, now derelict, mill. A pleasant scene.

The broad-fronted family pub has been here since about 1500 and part of it used to be the village jail. It is alleged that ghosts are around – footsteps have been heard from time to time and inexplicable temperature changes have been experienced. The thick stone walls of the old pub are decorated with brassware and some old horse harnesses. Lloyd-loom basket chairs are set around many small tables making for a relaxed atmosphere.

Among the wide variety of food available are chicken goujons with garlic, lamb chops, roast beef and Yorkshire pudding, chilli con carne, spaghetti Bolognese, salmon steak in parsley butter, chicken breasts and various steaks. To follow, there are such sweets as hot Dutch apple flan, treacle sponge, chocolate surprise, orange pompadour, Elton Snapper (no, it's not fish – try it!) and banana boat. Meals are served both at lunchtime and in the evening throughout the week. Everards Beacon and Wadworth Farmer's Glory are the real ales on offer. Children are welcomed. There is a special menu for them and they will find some swings in the pleasant garden. Dogs are not allowed in the pub, but will enjoy the garden, too.

Telephone: 01832 280240.

How to get there: Elton is 6 miles west of Peterborough. From the A1 some 2 miles north of the Norman Cross roundabout, take the slip road to the A605 towards Oundle. In 3 miles turn right to Elton, and the Black Horse is on the left in ½ mile.

Parking: The pub has a large car park on the opposite side of the road.

Length of the walk: 1½ miles or 3¾ miles. OS map: Landranger sheet 142 Peterborough and surrounding area (inn GR 089935).

After going past the church to Chapel Lane, the walk passes beside the gently rising broad expanse of Elton Park on a bridleway from which there are occasional glimpses of the river Nene, to the edge of the Northamptonshire village of Warmington. The way continues along wide headland paths across farmland back to Elton, passing the entrance to Elton Hall, just before the Black Horse. A short 1½ mile walk through the village to the river and the lock is also described.

The Walk

Leave the Black Horse and turn left towards the village. In about 100 yards turn left again, enter the churchyard and pass the south porch of All Saints' church. Swing right and leave the churchyard through a gate on the north side onto a tarmac road. After some 50 yards, turn left, go over a stile into a meadow and continue, with the school playing field fence on your right.

Keep straight on across the middle of a field to cross a two-step stile in a fence on the far side, then go through a small paddock

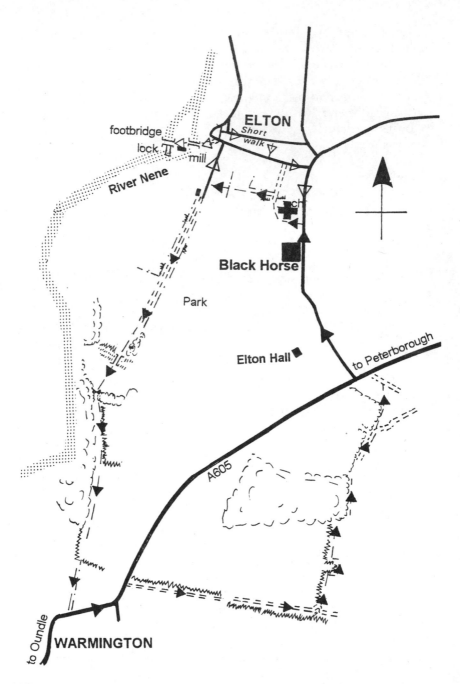

with isolated trees and over another two-step stile beside a gate to the road.

For the short walk to the village and the lock, turn right here and follow the directions at the end of the chapter.

For the full walk through Elton Park, turn left along Chapel Lane and, where the surfacing ends, at Acceber Cottage, go forward on a farm track, between fences with occasional short lengths of hedge. On the left is Elton Park where isolated specimen trees stand proudly amongst the grass and arable fields. Go through a gate and a few yards beyond it, where the fence on the right makes a right-angled turn, continue on a grassy path with a fence on the left. In the field beyond are elements of a point to point course.

Keep on the wide, grassy band, following the edge of the field and, as it swings slightly right, pass a few trees on the left. Away to the right there is a stand of tall timber.

When you come to a wooden bridge with two stiles, one each side, over a dry ditch which forms the county boundary, cross it and go straight ahead, climbing a slight hill through a pasture towards a tree belt. At the top go through a small gate into the woods.

In about 50 yards go through a wicket gate beside a cart gate and continue on a wide, grassy, leafy lane, with a hedge on the left and a belt of trees on the right. Pass a field boundary coming in on the left and keep in the same direction along the headland path, with woods on the right which slope down steeply to the bank of the river Nene. Ahead is the spire of Warmington church.

At the corner of a field, leave by a small gate and continue beside a fence on the left through a field which slopes down towards the river, a field away. Leave by a bridle gate beside the farm gate and reach a busy road, the A605.

Carefully cross to a footway and turn left. Go over Buntings Lane and continue, now on the wide grass verge of Peterborough Road. After 150 yards or so, at a footpath sign, turn right along a farm road, with a hedge on the left. In about ¼ mile the farm road changes to the other side of the hedge. Another ¼ mile further on you go through a gap in a cross-hedge and, at a waymark, turn left along a bridleway, on a broad headland with a hedge on the left.

At the corner of the field do a dog-leg right and left, pass over

The river Nene at Elton.

a timber bridge and through a hedge, and then in a few yards turn left. Follow the headland round to the right. Turn right again at the next field corner and keep beside a wood on the left. Go left at the corner, still on a grassy headland beside the trees.

In about 200 yards pass a number of fine mature oaks, with a few young trees among them, in a small pasture on the right. Just beyond the oak trees the grassy headland becomes a cinder track.

Quite soon, a short track joins from a field 50 yards away on the left. Here, where the cinder track makes a bend to the right, keep almost straight on, leaving the track, and follow a narrow path beside the wood on the left. Go through a small gate and continue in the same direction across a pasture to another gate in a fence on the far side, which leads to a surfaced farm road. Turn left and walk out to the main road.

Carefully cross over and go left. Turn right almost immediately on the road to Elton and return to the start.

For the short walk to the river Nene and the lock, follow the main route, as described from the Black Horse, past the church to Chapel Lane, and turn right. Pass a number of stone cottages on this narrow road, some of them thatched, and come to Middle Street at a T-junction, beside the chapel. Turn left.

Where the road turns right to Nassington, go left on a gravel path, immediately before a large chestnut tree. Pass through a small pedestrian gate, then swing right and follow a stone wall on the right. Go over a footbridge across a wide drainage channel, passing the derelict mill buildings on the left, and reach a bridge over the river Nene beside the lock.

Beyond the bridge there is a pleasant riverside area of grassland, generally cut for hay, managed sympathetically to encourage different plants and animals. It is a place of open access.

Having seen the lock, the river Nene and the riverside meadow, return the way you came, to the chestnut tree. Cross Middle Street and go towards Nassington. In 50 yards turn right. After 250 yards or so, opposite Hayes Walk on the left, turn right onto a narrow tarmac footpath. In a few yards walk down a steep ramp to the post office and the village stores. Turn left, walk to the T-junction and then go right, back to the Black Horse.

Places of interest nearby
Elton Hall, a large country house, rebuilt about 1660 with later additions, is open to the public from 2 pm to 5 pm on bank holiday Sundays and Mondays at Easter, May and August, plus Wednesdays and Sundays in July and Wednesdays, Thursdays and Sundays in August. Telephone: 01832 280468.

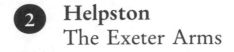

2 Helpston
The Exeter Arms

Helpston is an attractive village in the far north-west of Cambridgeshire. Pretty thatched cottages, surrounded by a riot of flowers in midsummer, look up to the church by the crossroads. Cows lean over the wall to watch you read the inscription on the memorial to local poet John Clare, while a few yards down the road is the cottage where he lived.

The Exeter Arms, in the shadow of the church, has an interesting history. On the first floor was once the court room, where the notorious Judge Jeffreys presided, while down below, to the right of the main door were the cells. To the left of the entrance is the area that, long ago, was the mortuary – note the great width of the door of the room, to get the coffins in and out. John Clare's mortal remains rested there after his death in 1864. Each of the two bars has a large fireplace, and next to the fire in the one-time mortuary is a big copper cauldron. Several dining tables are in the bar to the left of the door, and also one or two in the other bar which, at the far end, contains a pool table.

The range of food available will please all tastes. Sirloin, rump and gammon steaks, mixed grill, fisherman's pie, fillet of plaice or haddock, cheese and spinach lasagne, exotic bean and vegetable chilli, country bake pasta or deep-fried Brie with cranberry sauce are all on offer, and such sweets as home-made bread and butter pudding, chocolate fudge cake, fruit trifle and apple pie and cream can round off the meal. There are also special weeks devoted to one food, for instance a sausage week, when you can choose from Rutland sausage, pork and Stilton sausage or Lincolnshire sausage. John Smith's real ale and one guest beer are always available, as is Strongbow draught cider. Children are very welcome, and they have their own menu. On warm days they will appreciate the garden, which is well-equipped with play apparatus. The inn is open for drinking and meals at lunchtime and in the evening every day of the week. On Saturday and Sunday it is open all day. If well-behaved, dogs are allowed inside.

Telephone: 01733 252483.

How to get there: From Peterborough, go north on the A15 towards Market Deeping. Turn left on the B1443 for about a mile to reach Helpston. Turn right at the war memorial to find the Exeter Arms on the left.

From the south, follow the A1 to Wansford and the interchange with the A47. Take the A47 towards Peterborough and Wisbech. In 2 miles, at a roundabout, turn right for Ailsworth and in a mile, in Ailsworth, turn left for Helpston, which is reached in about 4 miles. At the war memorial, go straight on to the Exeter Arms.

Parking: There is plenty of parking at the rear of the pub.

Length of the walk: 3½ miles. OS map: Landranger sheet 142 Peterborough and surrounding area (inn GR 121056).

The walk starts through the attractive stone-built village, passing John Clare's house, which is privately owned. It subsequently follows a narrow path through Rice Wood and continues on to the tiny village of Ashton, returning by headland and cross-field paths to Helpston. The route coincides with two short stretches of the Torpel Way, a footpath running between Stamford and Peterborough.

The Walk

From the Exeter Arms turn right and walk down the road, with the church on the left. At the crossroads go straight over, past the war memorial, into Woodgate. Pass John Clare's house on the right and, shortly after, the Blue Bell. In about 200 yards, at the junction with Broad Wheel Road, keep left and continue along the road for about 1/4 mile.

Immediately after the last house on the right go right at a footpath sign, over a stile, and continue on a grassy headland beside a hedge on the right. Reach the corner of a wood and bear round to the left along the headland for about 10 yards. At a waymark, go right, cross a good footbridge and go over a stile into the trees. The narrow footpath meanders between the rows of pines with oaks interspersed.

Eventually cross a sleeper bridge onto a forest ride, but go straight over the ride and continue along a narrow path in the same direction as before. In a few yards cross over a minor forest track and keep on this narrow, winding footpath through the wood.

At the end of the trees cross a stile and a wooden footbridge over a ditch. Go straight on for about 100 yards on a cross-field path then, at the far side of the field, go right on a good headland path with a deep ditch on the left. This is the Torpel Way.

In about 100 yards pass an old stone barn on the left. Go through a gap in a cross-hedge by a footpath sign. A path on the right leads to Broad Wheel Road, but keep straight on along the Torpel Way, following a ditch on the left. Pass an electricity pylon on the right and continue beside the ditch on the left along this well-used headland path. Cross a wide wooden cart bridge, built in 1985 by the Peterborough Community Programme, and continue for 200 yards beside a deep ditch on the left to reach a minor road opposite Hilly Wood.

Go right along the road to the corner of the wood and then turn left on a well-used gravel farm road, signed to Ufford. Keep on the track, beside Hilly Wood. Later there is a hedge on the left but about 100 yards further on this changes to the right side of the track. As you walk admire the fine view. Just left of straight ahead you can see the spire of Barnack church.

At the end of the track, go over a stile beside a gate and turn right along a narrow country road with a wide verge on the right. In about 1/4 mile reach the small village of Ashton. Close to a bend

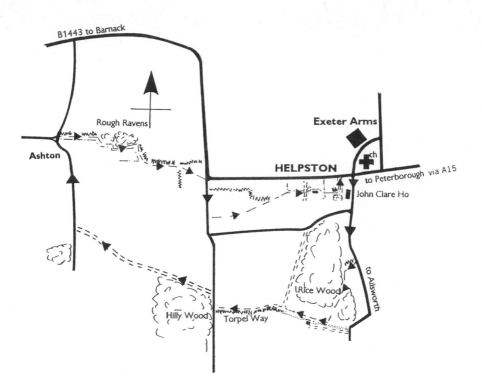

in the road, pass Gamekeeper's Cottage, a fine, renovated stone house. Keep right at the road junction with a grassy triangle, passing the entrance to Manor Farm on the right.

Immediately after the junction turn right at a footpath sign, along a further section of the Torpel Way. This is a narrow footpath between a hedge on the left and a wire fence. As you pass the farm on the right, look back to see the fine stone barn, now sympathetically converted to dwellings. Continue on this footpath beside fenced paddocks on the right and swing right to pass a small wood, Rough Ravens, on the left.

At the corner of the wood turn right, following a hedge on the left. Soon reach the far corner of the fenced paddock. Here continue on a very broad headland, still following the hedge on the left, which is gradually curving round to the left. Go over a stile at the corner of the field and turn half-right, away from the hedge you've been following up to now. Cross the rough pasture, keeping just to the right of the electricity pylon. After the pylon make for a stile in the hedge in front of you, and go out to a minor road at a T-junction.

Turn right. In about 300 yards from the road junction, and about 20 yards before a pylon in the field on your left, look for a waymark on a stick beside the road and turn left onto a cross-field path.

The line of the path is roughly towards the left-hand side of a line of bungalows which you can see in the distance and about 50 yards to the right of the end of a row of poplar trees. Across this large arable field, the path eventually reaches the end of a hedge on the left, and ahead is another field. Keep almost straight on along a continuation of the cross-field path to reach a corner of the field, just by the right-hand end of the row of poplars mentioned previously.

Continue beside the fence of the school playing field, on the left, then cross straight over a tarmac track at right angles. There is a stile here. Go across a piece of open grassland on a well-trodden path, bearing, at first, slightly right and passing a few trees on the left, then swing left on a well-used path, passing a steel silo and iron shed on the right.

After passing the iron buildings, cross a yard and then, moving slightly to the right, find, in the corner, a stone stile in a dry-stone wall, which leads to a broad, grassy path through more rough pasture. Keep straight on for a few yards and then follow a high hedge on the left. In about 15 yards there is a path on the right, but keep on for another 10 yards and then turn left on a narrow footpath between hedges, out to the road.

Turn right and in 100 yards turn left towards the church and the Exeter Arms.

Places of interest nearby

A thriving John Clare Society organises the annual Clare Festival, held in Helpston each July, and arranges exhibitions, poetry readings and conferences celebrating Clare's life, poetry and birthday on 13 July, 1793. To find out more about the John Clare Society, ring the Secretary, Mrs Mary Moyse on 01733 252678.

3 Ferry Meadows, Peterborough
The Granary

The river Nene flows through Peterborough, and to the west of the city, beside the river, is Nene Park, a 6 mile long recreational area owned and managed by the Nene Park Trust. At the centre of Nene Park is Ferry Meadows, a 500 acre country park opened in 1978. A wide variety of water-based activities are catered for on its lakes and there is a nature reserve, as well as informal grassed areas for play. Ferry Meadows is criss-crossed with paths, the majority of which are surfaced ways suitable for wheelchairs.

The Granary, which is very close to the edge of the Country Park, is unusual in that wherever one sits in this attractive building there is an intimate feeling, as there are lots of small areas, on several different levels – almost like a stage-set of a village, for the various parts have their own roofs, within the pub.

On the menu you will find sirloin, rump, T bone or peppered steak, chicken Oscar, marinated chicken or chicken tikka masala, ocean bake, beef and Boddingtons pie, provençale nut Wellington and pasta lucana and much more. Follow that with your choice from, among others, profiterole surprise, horn of plenty, brandysnap corruption, strawberry pavlova and tiramisu cake. Boddingtons, Flowers IPA, Abbot Ale and two guests are always available, as are Strongbow and Merrydown draught cider. Children are very welcome. A menu is specially designed for them and in the garden are swings and a climbing frame. Dogs are allowed in the garden, but not inside the pub. The Granary is open all day, every day of the week and meals are served throughout opening times.

Telephone: 01733 235794.

How to get there: From the south, follow the A1 northward towards Peterborough. Keep straight on at the Norman Cross roundabout and go past the junction for the A1139 (signed 'Peterborough'). In a further mile or so take a slip road signed for the Showground, Chesterton and Alwalton. Shortly, at a T-junction, turn left, signed 'A605 Peterborough', and follow brown 'Nene Park' signs, straight over three roundabouts, and then bear left on a minor road signed 'Ferry Meadows'. Turn right into Ham Lane and the Granary is on the left.

From Peterborough and from points due west, follow 'Nene Park' and then 'Ferry Meadows' signs.

The Nene Valley Railway between Peterborough and Yarwell Junction runs just to the south of Ferry Meadows and there is a station to serve the area.

Parking: There is a large car park beside the Granary and, in addition, there is a good car park (a charge is made on summer weekends and bank holidays) in Ferry Meadows, Ham Lane.

Length of the walk: 3¾ miles, or 2½ miles if you take the short-cut. OS map: Landranger sheet 142 Peterborough and surrounding area (inn GR 154967).

The walk is along good, well-maintained paths through the Ferry Meadows Country Park. These are not on the definitive map of rights of way but are maintained by the Nene Park Trust and are open at all times, although the park is closed to vehicles during the hours of darkness.

After crossing the Nene Valley Railway, the walk goes through a nature reserve, passing two bird hides. Over the river Nene, the path climbs through riverside bluebell woods to Milton Ferry Bridge. The return is along well-used and surfaced paths beside lakes used for boating, sailing and fishing, passing a visitors' centre.

The Walk

From the Granary go out to the road and turn right along Ham Lane. Go over to the opposite footway. Just after the road crosses a broad ditch, take the surfaced path, which swings left and continues parallel to Ham Lane, signed 'Ferry Meadows'. In about 300 yards this returns to the road at a level crossing of the Nene Valley Railway. A few yards further on turn right along a surfaced path, signed 'Station, Orton Mere and City Centre'.

Passing the station, keep beside the railway and shortly cross a timber bridge over a wide ditch. Continue on the surfaced path and, where it bends round to the right, turn sharp left and cross the arched timber bridge to enter the nature reserve through a pedestrian gate. Quietly walk on the gravel path between a watercourse on the right and a willow thicket on the left. A little further on, there are a few boats moored and, nearby, the channel joins the river Nene.

Pass, on the left, the Ian Prest Hide, from which the wildfowl on a secluded scrape, or lake, can be observed. Ahead you can see Bluebell Bridge over the Nene, which will be crossed later. Continue on the gravel path, turning left and following the bank of a waterway which links with the lakes. Notice on the left the John Peake Hide, another place to see the wildlife undisturbed. At the end of the reserve, bear to the right and cross the water by a bridge. From this point there is a choice.

For the shorter walk, bear round to the left at the junction of tracks and follow the shore of Overton Lake on the left until you reach the footbridge, which is easily identified because the centre section floats on a pontoon, and rejoin the main walk.

For the full walk, bear right at the junction of paths, walk to Bluebell Bridge and cross the river Nene. Keep straight on along a tarmac path, with woods on the left. In a little over 100 yards go left on a broad gravel path through mixed woodlands. Keep straight on where a wide path goes right. Eventually the way swings left, down towards the river. Continue, still in woodland beside the river, until you reach the stone Milton Ferry Bridge.

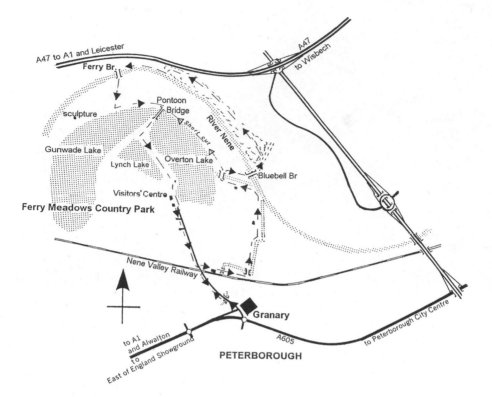

Cross the bridge and keep straight on along a tarmac path to reach the edge of Gunwade Lake. Observe, to the right, on a slight rise less than ¼ mile away, John Maine's sculpture, *Pyramid*.

Turn left on the tarmac path beside Gunwade Lake, which in just over a ¼ mile narrows to a strait leading to Overton Lake, another large boating area. At a junction, take the path to the right and cross the pontoon bridge. This is where those who have taken the short-cut rejoin the main walk.

Some 100 yards beyond the bridge turn left at a sign, 'To Roman Point and the Visitors' Centre'. Cross a timber bridge and you are now on a neck of land beside Lynch Lake, with the larger Overton Lake behind a belt of trees on the left of the path.

At the end of Lynch Lake, join a path coming in on the right and almost immediately turn left, just near the wooden sculpture

'Song of Sisyphus' by Doug Cocker.

Song of Sisyphus by Doug Cocker. Follow this narrower path to reach Roman Point, the site of a Roman dwelling, and continue along the path, soon passing a children's play area. Keep on the broad tarmac road past the visitors' centre on the right, and take a footway beside the roadside verge on the right. Cross the level crossing and retrace your steps to the Granary.

Places of interest nearby
As well as the two sculptures at Ferry Meadows, seen on the walk, there are several other modern pieces in Nene Park, just to the east at *Thorpe Meadows.* There are 32 exhibits of sculpture in and around Peterborough, looked after by the Peterborough Sculpture Trust. *Peterborough City and Cathedral* can be reached by footpaths and cycleways through Nene Park. *The Nene Valley Railway* runs from Peterborough westwards beyond Wansford to Yarwell Junction. The return trip is 15 miles and there are intermediate stations at Ferry Meadows and Orton Mere. At Wansford there is a collection of historic locomotives and coaches, and Thomas the Tank Engine can sometimes be seen. For full details and timetable ring 01780 782854.

23

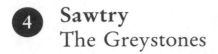

4 Sawtry
The Greystones

The line of the Great North Road, which lies just east of the village, almost forms the edge of the extensive fenland stretching eastward through Ramsey across north-east Cambridgeshire to Ely and Wisbech. In contrast, the landscape to the west of Sawtry is of little valleys and small, rounded hills, which are sufficiently elevated to provide good and interesting views. Sawtry itself is a large and busy village, at the centre of which is a broad green around which some older houses are clustered.

The Greystones pub, shaded by trees, stands on a corner site in the heart of Sawtry facing the village green. The broad-fronted welcoming pub has a wide bar area, from which two big bay windows with tables in each recess, look out to tables and benches set in the garden under sun umbrellas, in season. There is also a beer garden to one side of the pub. The menu lists various steaks, gammon, egg and pineapple, fisherman's platter, ham and eggs, chicken fillets, cheese and vegetable bake and a possible 15 different fillings for toasted 4 inch baps. For dessert you are offered lemon pudding, jam roly-poly, spotted dick and apple or cherry pie and cream. Boddingtons real ale is served, plus a guest beer, and Blackthorn and Bulmer's cider are available. Children are welcome – there is a special menu, with little fishes, miniburgers, chicken nuggets and dinosaurs, to please them and a play area outside. Dogs, if well-behaved, are allowed inside the pub, but not in the garden. The Greystones is open all day from Monday to Saturday, and at the usual Sunday times. No food is served on Sunday evenings.

Telephone: 01487 831999.

How to get there: Sawtry is just off the A1, about 4 miles north of the Alconbury interchange with the northern spur of the A14. Take the signed turning to the village, where you will find the Greystones in the centre.

Parking: There is ample parking at the pub and also some additional space nearby in the village.

Length of the walk: 4½ miles. OS map: Landranger sheet 142 Peterborough and surrounding area (inn GR 167837).

The walk circles Aversley Wood, which in Saxon times formed part of a long belt of woodland stretching north–south beside the waterlogged fens. Visitors are welcome in the wood, which is owned by the Woodland Trust, and an information board is displayed.

At first the walk is along headland and cross-field paths, rising up a hill to reach Bullock Road, a long, straight byway which at one time was the route for driving cattle to market in Bedford. It runs alongside Aversley Wood, at the corner of which was a pond where animals in transit were watered. The return is by means of a grassy path across High Holborn Hill, back to the village.

The Walk

From the Greystones turn left and take Gidding Road (signed 'Hamerton' and 'Giddings'). After passing Westfield Road on the left and Deerpark Road on the right, the footway ends but you continue along the broad verge on the right-hand side of the road. Pass an isolated house and just before you reach a farm on the

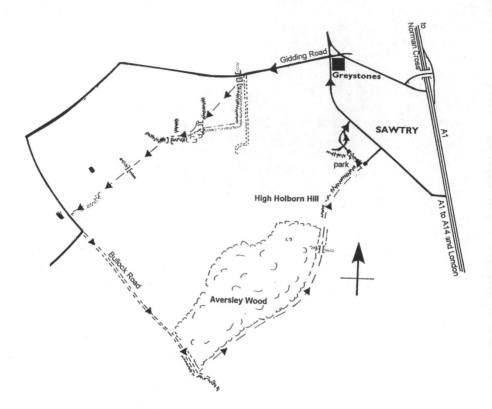

right, and a small road bridge with steel railings, turn left onto a concrete farm track. Immediately (in 5 yards) turn right across a timber footbridge and enter a field.

Cross the field diagonally, as indicated by the waymark on the bridge handrail, and at the corner go over a stile, followed by a plank bridge. Turn left and walk along a headland path with a ditch and hedge on the left. Go through a broad gap in a. cross-hedge and in 20 yards go left over a substantial wooden bridge. Turn right for 15 yards beside a tall hedge on the right. Where the hedge makes a bend half-right, keep straight on as shown by the waymark, climbing on a cross-field path.

As you ascend, look back over Sawtry and the Cambridgeshire Fens beyond. Go through a cross-hedge and over a two-sleeper footbridge and continue on a reinstated cross-field path. After passing Woodfield Farm away to the right, you reach a pond near the top of the hill.

Follow the pond round to the left and then swing right at the field boundary and walk alongside the shallow ditch on the left. Where this ends go straight on across a field towards a row of trees to the left of Cold Harbour Farm and, by a footpath sign, turn left along a road at the crest of the hill, from where you can look both left and right to see wide stretches of countryside.

In 100 yards or so, where the tarmac road bends sharply right towards Hamerton Wildlife Centre, keep straight on towards the woods, along Bullock Road, a grassy byway, following, at first, a line of telephone poles. Halfway along this path, pass barns and sheds, about 100 yards away on the right. Continue to Aversley Wood on the left and a Woodland Trust entrance gate. If you have time to explore, you can go through the wood, and exit on the east side, somewhere near the north corner.

Follow straight on the broad, grassy track alongside, on the left, the mixed wood with oak, ash and hawthorn. Soon the track gets narrower and there is a ditch on the right. At the end of the wood, go through a gap in a cross-hedge and leave the byway, Bullock Road, turning left on a wide, grassy headland path beside the wood on the left.

Continue downhill by the wood, passing several cross-hedges and ditches. Eventually, at a low point, cross a narrow stream by a wide footbridge. Just past here, on the left, is another public entrance to the wood and an information board.

Climb a hill on a wide grass path, with a post and wire fence on the right. Almost at the top of High Holborn Hill, where the wood on the left ends, continue in the same direction, following a sparse hedge.

Descend the hill on a grass path, with the hedge on the left and, later, some allotments on the right, and go over a stile onto a small car park at the entrance to the recreation ground.

Turn left across the head of the car park and take the concrete path through the recreation ground. After crossing a ditch, continue on a narrow tarmac path to the head of a cul-de-sac.

Walk along the road to a crossroads. Turn right and keep along Rockingham Road to its end at a T-junction. Turn left and walk back about 1/2 mile to the Greystones.

A cottage in Sawtry.

Places of interest nearby

Hamerton Wildlife Centre is about 3 miles south-west of Sawtry. Open daily, except for Christmas, from 10.30 am till 6 pm (4 pm in winter). Telephone: 01832 293362. *Holme Fen Nature Reserve* is about 4 miles north-east of Sawtry, on the eastern side of the A1. Here you can see the fascinating Holme Fen Posts, which show dramatically how the fenland has shrunk since the drainage of the fens began in the 17th century. The land has dropped over 13 ft in that time due to the shrinkage of the peat as it dried out.

St Neots
The Bridge House

The small, bustling town of St Neots lies on the banks of the river Great Ouse, which flows northward to Huntingdon. Close beside the river, and the town's bridge, lies a broad square, given over to stalls on Thursdays, market day.

The many gabled Bridge House stands on the bank of the river beside the bridge. The restaurant overlooks the river, and down below is a terrace with tables and chairs where customers may watch the leisure craft chugging up and down the broad waterway. The building is a rambling succession of rooms on different levels, making for an interesting pub.

To stimulate the taste buds before or after a walk, you can choose from such dishes as rump, sirloin, fillet or T-bone steak, chicken or sirloin Oscar, minted lamb steak or red snapper Florentine. Among the sweets are horn of plenty, profiterole surprise, Mississippi steamboat and fresh fruit salad. As for drinks, Flowers Original, Boddingtons and a guest ale are served, together with Strongbow draught cider. Children are welcome and are offered a Mr Men menu with a tempting range. If aged 3 to 15 months they can have free baby food. The inn is open all day, every day. Restaurant meals are available at lunchtime and in the evening on Monday to Friday and all day on Saturday and Sunday. Dogs are not allowed inside.

Telephone: 01480 472044.

How to get there: The main road between Cambridge and Bedford used to cross the river Great Ouse at the centre of St Neots. Today the A428, its successor, bypasses the town. Consequently, leave the A428 at the 'St Neots' signs and go straight on to the town centre. The Bridge House is close by the Market Square, and beside the bridge.

Parking: Although the pub can offer no parking there is a large car park just 100 yards away over the river bridge, at Riverside Park (turn sharp left at the roundabout).

Length of the walk: 2³/₄ miles. OS map: Landranger sheet 153 Bedford, Huntingdon and surrounding area (inn GR 181602).

The walk goes south from the town, passing Brook House, a handsome Georgian building, and the parish church of St Mary, then on an attractive riverside path to Eaton Socon Lock, close to a former mill. In the 17th century, locks were built downstream so that navigation as far as the sea was possible. The return is amid farmland scenery to Eynesbury and, after crossing the river on a modern footbridge, through Riverside Park back to St Neots Bridge.

The Walk

From the Bridge House cross the road and make your way to the diagonally opposite corner of the Market Square, then go out along a narrow road and turn right into South Street. Follow the road as it goes left, passing Brook House and St Mary's church, then go right into Church Street and over the bridge.

At a road junction pass the church of St Mary the Virgin, Eynesbury, on your left and continue, going round slowly to your right with an open space on the right. See, on the left, the modern looking Coney Geare public house and opposite it

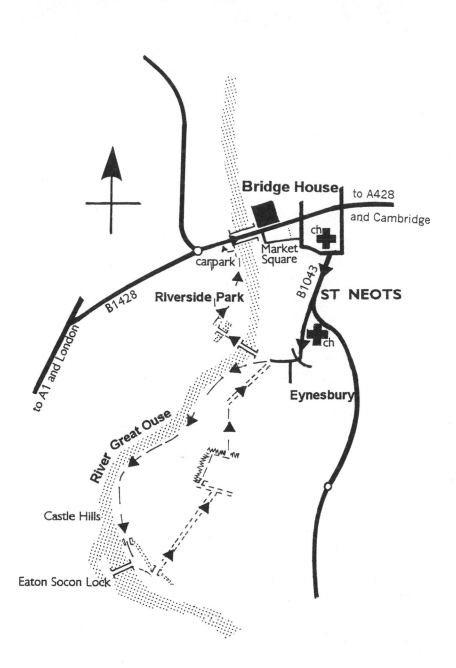

Bridge House

to A428
and Cambridge

carpark

Market
Square

ch

B1428

to A1 and London

Riverside Park

B1043

ST NEOTS

ch

Eynesbury

River Great Ouse

Castle Hills

Eaton Socon Lock

a children's play area. Pass a footpath on the right leading to a pair of footbridges, which you will return to later, and in a few yards reach a car park and, partway along it, turn right on a narrow footpath and go down towards the river's edge.

Go left and wander along beside the water through light woodland, with willows and summertime marsh marigolds. Continue, now with a well-tended grassy area on the left. After going over two small footbridges, you will see Castle Hills on the opposite bank, and then River Mill with its marina.

Cross a substantial wooden footbridge, then go up and over the steps beside the weir, which belongs to the Great Ouse River Authority. Swing left away from the river on a surfaced footpath through light woodland and bear left to cross a broad timber bridge to a large field. Follow a wide hardcore track heading directly towards the distant church.

At a T-junction of tracks turn left on a wide, grassy path and in 100 yards bear right over a culvert and snake right then left, with a hedge on the left. At the corner of the field go right, still with a ditch and hedge on the left. Presently turn left through the hedge-cum-shelter belt into a smallish triangular field on a well-worn path that leads to the apex and on between a fence and a hedge. At the entrance to the camping site bear right along the access road to reach the car park you passed earlier.

Swing left before the children's play area and take the footbridge across the Great Ouse to Riverside Park. In a few yards cross another footbridge and turn right on a tarmac path which roughly follows a small backwater of the river. Cross another bridge, passing boating lakes, and come to a quay where river trips sometimes operate.

On reaching the road bridge and viaduct, go left, away from the river, turn right under the road and climb steps up to the footway on the north side of the bridge. Keep on over the bridge to return to the start.

Places of interest nearby
From the Riverside car park river trips can be taken on Saturdays, Sundays and bank holidays.

6 Brampton
The Olde Mill

Brampton, the birthplace of Samuel Pepys, is situated to the west of Huntingdon, beside the river Great Ouse. A few miles further west lies the large lake of Grafham Water.

The theme of this idyllic, remote, part weather-boarded riverside pub, with its long river frontage where terns swoop over the water, with a landing stage alongside, is fishing. Ranged around the walls are fishing rods, nets, baskets, fish kettles and paintings of river scenes. The Domesday Book mentioned a mill here. There are many changes of level and in the bar are two glass tables, placed directly over the water as it flows under the pub.

Many different steaks are available, and examples of other dishes are marinated chicken, provençale nut Wellington, Indonesian chicken, pasta lucana and ocean bake. Children are made welcome and they have their own menu. For the really tinies there is free baby food, both sweet and savoury. Several resident real ales are on offer, such as Wadworth 6X, Boddingtons Bitter, Flowers Original, Castle Eden and Brakspear Bitter. Strongbow draught cider and Merrydown are also available. The inn is open all day, every day. Meals are served at lunchtime and in the evening on Monday to Friday and throughout opening hours at the weekend. Dogs are not allowed inside the inn. The proximity of the water calls for extra vigilance if you have small children with you.

Telephone: 01480 459758.

How to get there: Following the A14, at the two-level intersection west of Huntingdon, take the slip road and continue on the A14 towards Kettering. Leave at the next slip road, signed for Brampton. Head towards Huntingdon, taking the first exit at the roundabout near the centre of the village. In ½ mile turn right onto a minor road called Bromholme Lane, and after passing a marina on the left follow the single track road to reach the Olde Mill.

Parking: There is parking alongside the river by the pub.

Length of the walk: 2¾ miles. OS map: Landranger sheet 153 Bedford, Huntingdon and surrounding area (inn GR 224707).

This short, easy walk starts over the golf course and then crosses several meadows to Brampton church. After a little distance along a village street, the return is down a quiet lane to the river Great Ouse and then along the bank, finally going through woodlands and passing a lock on the far side.

The Walk

From the Olde Mill walk back along the access road. Pass a lane off to the left, signed 'Public Footpath Ouse Valley Way', and then the marina on the right. Soon, at a junction, the Ouse Valley Way goes right. Almost immediately afterwards, and before the first house on the left, go left on a narrow footpath leading to the golf course, between an old hedge on the right and a fence on the left.

Go through a kissing-gate and bear right across the golf course, making for a point beyond the right-hand side of an old military building. The route is marked by a pair of blue sticks. At the edge of the course go through another kissing-gate and carry straight on out to the road. Go left for 15 yards, crossing the drive to

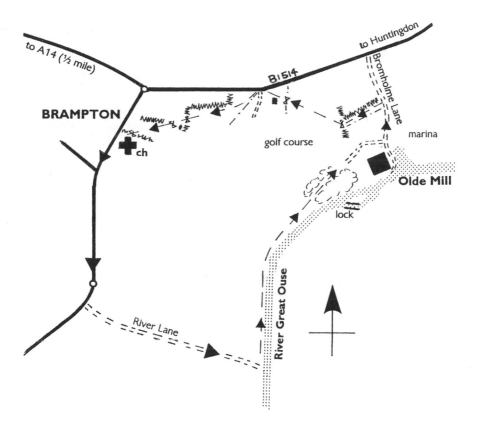

'Water Meadows', and then go left at a sign, through yet another kissing-gate, following at first a steel fence on the left.

Soon bear away from the steel fence towards the corner of some gardens on the right. Keep on towards a gap in the hedge and then continue in roughly the same direction through kissing-gates and across pastures and eventually enter the churchyard. Pass the north door of the church and go out and turn left along the road.

Pass the Black Bull on the left, and High Street on the right. Soon reach a roundabout at the entrance to the Brampton RAF Station. Go straight on but in a few yards turn left into River Lane, a narrow tarmac road.

When the tarmac ends, continue along the narrow gravel track, with the golf course on the left. At the end, after the golf course, turn left at a T-junction of tracks.

The river Great Ouse.

This is a hard, well-walked path beside the wide river Great Ouse and is part of the Ouse Valley Way. After following the river as it bends to the right, move slightly away from the water, walking through a plantation of willows on a good, well-defined track, keeping roughly parallel to the river on the right. On the far side there are sluices and a lock. Eventually join a concrete track.

When you come to a red steel gate across the track go left for a few yards, and at a waymark pass through a gap in the fence and turn back to the concrete track. Go over a bridge and continue on the hard track as it swings right in a big circle. On reaching the narrow single-track road go sharp right and follow it back to the Olde Mill and the start.

Places of interest nearby
Hinchingbrooke House, now a school, was at one time owned by Oliver Cromwell's family. It is open to the public on summer Sunday afternoons. *Grafham Water*, part of Anglia Water's storage system, is used for all manner of recreation and for wildlife conservation and many pleasant hours can be spent there.

7 Croydon
The Queen Adelaide

Croydon is an isolated village spread out along a minor road at the side of Croydon Hill. Behind the houses the land rises steeply to a summit plateau about 250 ft high. To the south lies a broad, flat valley, on the far side of which stands the Hertfordshire town of Royston.

The Queen Adelaide stands a long way back from the road on level ground with a hill rising behind it, and the land in front falling away to the Hertfordshire plain. The somewhat stark, four-square, slate-roofed black and white exterior belies a warm welcoming interior. The pub is large, but far from impersonal. Open stud partitioning subdivides it into smaller, more intimate areas. The establishment is called after the wife of King William IV, the name it has carried since 1831. Exposed dark beams and plenty of gleaming brass add character to the building.

Home-cooked food is the speciality here and it is renowned for miles around. In particular, pies such as chicken and ham, steak and kidney, rabbit and mushroom, Cambridgeshire game and Adelaide fisherman's should be mentioned. Vegetarians are catered for with leek, Stilton and potato bake and broccoli and cheese bake. Examples of the sweets are raspberry charlotte, super sundae, various cheesecakes, chocolate fudge cake and sticky toffee meringue. Children are welcome provided they are seated, dining with their parents. There is a special menu for them and they will enjoy the swings in the large garden. The ales served are Greene King IPA, Rayments and Boddingtons Bitter. Dry Blackthorn draught cider is on sale too. The pub is open for drinking and for food, both at lunchtime and in the evening, seven days a week. Dogs are allowed inside if well-behaved.

Telephone: 01223 208278.

How to get there: Croydon lies to the west of the A1198 Huntingdon to Royston road, about 7 miles south of the Caxton Gibbet roundabout, its junction with the A428 Cambridge to St Neots road. Turn right on a minor road almost opposite the Hardwicke Arms at Arrington. Croydon village and the Queen Adelaide are reached in 2 miles.

Parking: Beside and in front of the pub there is plenty of parking space.

Length of the walk: 3½ miles. OS map: Landranger sheet 153 Bedford, Huntingdon and surrounding area (inn GR 313493).

This pleasant and easy walk starts by climbing Croydon Hill on a broad farm road. At the top, the circuit continues along a well-used farm track over the plateau. The return is on headland paths and across pasture. On descending the hill to the Queen Adelaide, you have fine views over the flat valley to the chalk hills of Hertfordshire, 5 miles away.

The Walk

From the Queen Adelaide go left, soon passing All Saints' church on the left. At the war memorial, where a sign says 'The Clopton Way', turn left onto Church Lane and climb the hill beside the church.

In about 300 yards leave the waymarked Clopton Way and continue on the tarmac track which bends sharply left between

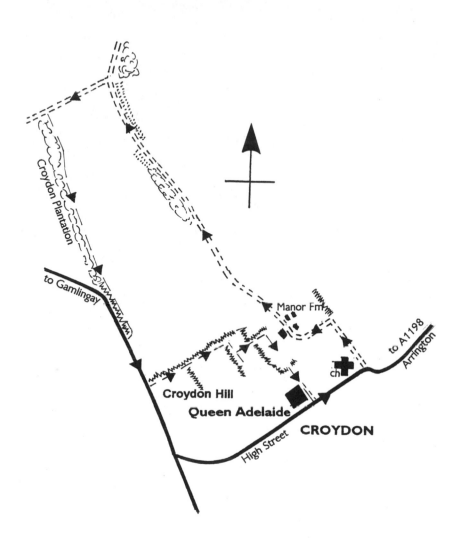

ranch-style fences and then swings gently round to the right. Pass a bungalow and walk on, through the farm. Keep straight on along a hardcore farm track with a wide verge which, in spring, is gay with clumps of daffodils.

Stay on the cart track, beside a hawthorn thicket 50 yards wide

Croydon Hill.

on the left, for about ¼ mile. Immediately after the thicket there is a deep ditch on the left. In 50 yards the track crosses the ditch and then continues, with the ditch and a hedge on the right. Where it makes a bend to the right, by the corner of a small oak wood on the right, turn left at a waymark on a grassy farm track with a hedge on the right.

At the far side of the field leave the cart track and go left at a waymark on a headland path with a belt of mixed woodland, called Croydon Plantation, on the right. Where the tree belt on the right ends, go right for 20 yards out to the road and turn left.

Just before the 'Steep Hill' sign, and at the next cross-hedge on the left, turn left on a wide grass path with a hedge on the left. You are walking on top of the hill. To the right the block-like buildings of Bassingbourn Barracks can be seen. At the field boundary go through a wide gap in the hedge and continue in the same direction on the wide grass path. Cross a stile beside a gate at the next field boundary, into a lovely meadow, and turn right and descend the hill.

Follow down beside the right-hand edge of the field for about 100 yards and, close to a waymark, turn left across the meadow, going through a waymarked gate on the opposite side. Continue on beside a hedge on the left until, in about 100 yards, you see, to your left, a stile. At this point, by a waymark, go right, across a pasture, roughly in line with an electricity pole. Walk downhill, then cross a stile in some rough ground and continue down a grassy path to the lane, which is beside an electricity sub-station and the pub.

Places of interest nearby
Wimpole Hall (National Trust), to the east of the A1198. This vast mansion and its large park and farm can all be visited between March and October, every day except Monday and Friday. The restaurant and shop stay open during the winter, and the Home Farm is also open at weekends in some winter months. Telephone 01223 207257 for details.

8 Fenstanton
The King William IV

At the heart of the village is an attractive brick-built clockhouse. It was constructed around 1650 and restored by the parish council in 1989. The guide to the interesting church of Saints Peter and Paul points out that visitors equipped with binoculars may see more of the rich carvings than those without. Will you spot the corbel that is a carving of a man with his tongue sticking out? Near the north wall of the chancel, outside, is a stone commemorating Lancelot 'Capability' Brown, the famed landscape gardener, born in 1715, who lived in the village. In 1770 he was High Sheriff of Huntingdon. He laid out many large gardens, notably Kew and Blenheim.

The King William IV, in the centre of Fenstanton, is a charming, long, low-beamed pub dating from the 17th century. The gleaming brass and a cheery wintertime log fire add to the atmosphere. On Wednesday evenings you will always find live blues or jazz music.

Whatever you choose to eat, you are in for culinary delights here. Lamb cutlets with a honey and garlic glaze, seafood pie with plaice, scallops, cockles and prawns, braised liver and onions, venison and walnut pie, asparagus and peanut strudel and leek and cheese crumble are but a few of the main dishes. As if that were not enough, you could also have, for example, Tia Maria cheesecake, brandysnaps, chocolate sponge or treacle and walnut tart. As for drinks, Greene King ales are the order of the day, or Red Rock cider. Children who can sit still are welcome! They may dine with their parents in the non-smoking restaurant, choosing from their own special menu. There is a garden area, too, beyond the restaurant. The King William is open all the usual hours each day of the week. Meals are served every lunchtime and evening. Well-behaved dogs may be brought into the pub.

Telephone: 01480 462467.

How to get there: Fenstanton is just off the A14 Cambridge to Huntingdon road, about 10 miles north-west of Cambridge. Take the signed slip road to the village. The King William IV is at the north-west end of the main street.

Parking: A little way along Chequers Street, which is opposite the pub, is the parish's free car park. Parking by the pub itself is possible, but a bit limited.

Length of the walk: 2³/₄ miles. OS map: Landranger sheet 153 Bedford, Huntingdon and surrounding area (inn GR 314684).

This short walk from Fenstanton is along easy and well-used paths across farmland to the banks of the Great Ouse. The river is an important waterway and you may see narrow boats and other craft sailing its waters.

The Walk
Cross the road from the King William and walk along Chequers Street, passing the parish car park on the left. Later pass a small triangular green in front of the United Reformed church on the right.

Although you will want to explore the village church at some point, for the purpose of the walk do not turn right into Church Lane, but continue straight on to reach Honey Hill, another

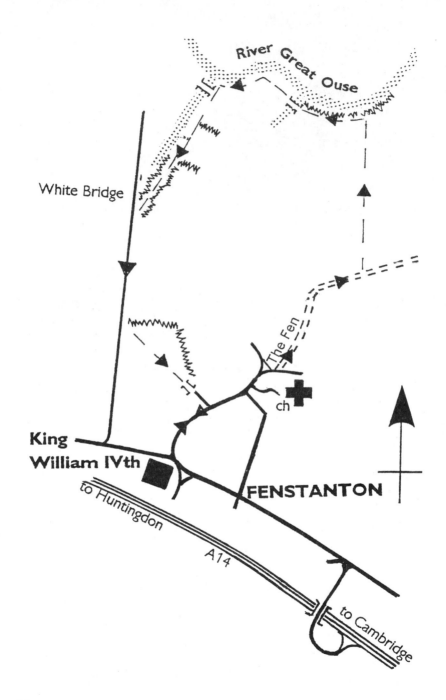

River Great Ouse

White Bridge

The Fen

ch

King
William IVth

FENSTANTON

to Huntingdon

A14

to Cambridge

triangular green. Keep the green on the left and, immediately after, swing slightly right and then go left into The Fen, an unmade road.

Pass a tarmac school playground on the right. Continue on the track, which bends round to the right, with a hedge and ditch on both sides. Soon there is a footpath off to the right and, 20 yards beyond, at another sign denoting a footpath off to the left, go left through a broken down gate. Head straight across the field on a grassy cart track and, at the far side, turn left on a headland path.

There is a hedge on the right, and just beyond it is the river Great Ouse. Cross a broad concrete bridge over a wide dyke, then a long narrow timber bridge and finally a stile which takes you onto the river bank. Straight ahead you can see St Ives church spire.

Continue to follow the river as it makes a sharp turn to the left. In about 200 yards, where the bank makes a bend to the right, there is a substantial bridge across a broad, deep drainage ditch feeding the river. Do not cross the bridge, but continue beside the ditch on the right. At the field boundary go over a stile and keep straight on. When you come to the next hedge, a stile beside a gate leads into a grassy cart track between hedges. At the end of the track go over a stile and turn left along a road.

Using the footway beside the road, pass Crystal Lakes Caravan Site and shortly after, at the footpath sign, go left to cross the field almost diagonally on a well-marked path, passing close to a cricket field and a mid-field electricity pole. As you go, you can see the tall spire of Fenstanton church half-left.

Cross a substantial, long timber bridge which leads into a narrow footpath. Go out through a steel kissing-gate and along a tarmac drive. When you reach the road opposite the Chequers, turn right, back to the start.

Places of interest nearby
Hilton Turf Maze. In the adjacent parish of Hilton, just over a mile away, is a large maze on the common, one of only eight surviving turf mazes in England. It was cut in 1660, the year in which King Charles II was restored to the throne. Hilton Parish Council carefully tend it.

9 Swavesey
The White Horse Inn

This is a peaceful place beside the river Great Ouse, about 7 miles from Cambridge. Gravel extraction work in the area has resulted in a number of lakes, now well restored and landscaped, on which many wildfowl feed, and angling is a major sport here.

The White Horse was built about 1620 to provide accommodation for the users of the dock, which was once just at the end of Market Street. This is a comfortable pub, with horse bits, hunting pictures and barrel taps adorning the walls.

The establishment prides itself on its home cooking, which has won several national awards. While 'Anthony's Steak and Kidney Pie' must be mentioned first, there are also curries, such as Burmese chicken curry, lamb gosht and three bean curry. Or you could have grilled lamb chops, lasagne or cheese and broccoli hot pot. Home-made apple pie, a pudding of the day, sorbets or banana split could follow. Real ales such as Old Speckled Hen, Boddingtons and Flowers IPA are in stock for liquid refreshment, as is Strongbow draught cider. Children dining with their parents are welcome and there is a garden for them to play in. The inn is open at lunchtime and in the evening, seven days a week, for both food and drink. Dogs are welcome if well-behaved.

Telephone: 01954 230239.

How to get there: From the A14 between Cambridge and Huntingdon take the turning, signed to Swavesey, by the Trinity Foot public house (some 3 miles from the M11 interchange). The White Horse is about 2 miles from the A14, at the northern end of the village's main street.

Parking: There is plenty of parking in the broad Market Street, just in front of the inn.

Length of the walk: 2½ miles. OS map: Landranger sheet 154 Cambridge, Newmarket and surrounding area (inn GR 361689).

The walk starts from the village green, which long ago was a dock. It was later filled in and grassed over but the cottage at the end is still called Dock Keepers Cottage. The route takes you beside a lake, the result of gravel workings, along the river Great Ouse and back by quiet lanes.

The Walk

Leave the White Horse and turn right to reach the junction of Station Street and Taylors Lane. Go left into Taylors Lane, bearing round to the right and going past a road on your left.

After passing the cemetery on your left, do not follow the main track round the corner, but keep straight on, along a broad gravel track. The footpath sign says 'Public Footpath Holywell 1½'. Cross the disused mineral railway line and continue towards the bend in the track ahead, on the limestone chip surface.

By the bend you will see Swavesey Lake, a restored gravel pit, on your right. Presently go up the slope towards Covell's Bridge, but before the bridge, turn right over a stile and walk, with a waterway on your left, for about 200 yards to a narrow footbridge.

The official right of way crosses the water to follow the west bank, and returns about 200 yards further on, by a concrete bridge, to the east bank of the wide channel. At the present

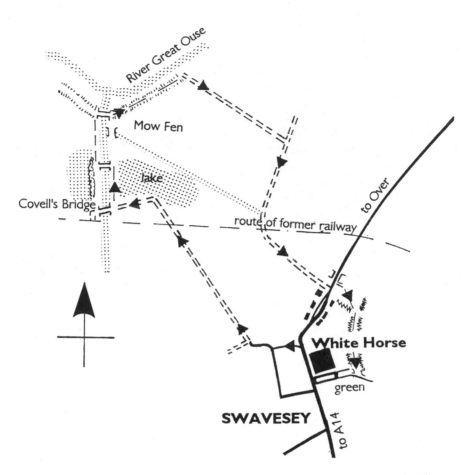

time, steel handrails designed to keep stock off the concrete bridge make it difficult for pedestrians, other than the adventurous, to use. However, in practice, people seem to avoid crossing either bridge. We understand the railings will be modified but until alterations are made, keep straight on, cross a stile and meet the flood protection bank of the river Great Ouse just by the bridge you have not used, which is alongside a pair of flood protection gates.

Turn right and continue beside the curving river, on a raised bank some 100 yards from the water's edge. You may well see swans, Canada geese, terns and great crested grebes.

At the end of the field go over a two-step stile. Do not cross

Swavesey village.

the next stile but turn right and drop down from the river wall into a grassy-middled green lane. Here there are many big willows with their characteristic grey-green narrow leaves. You come to a T-junction with a stony track. Go right, soon with a view of Swavesey church. Cross the old mineral line again and continue along the gravel track for about ¼ mile to meet a road at a T-junction.

Turn left, but before doing so have a look at the narrow, pleasant area between two roads on your right.

Walk to the left as far as the road bridge, and immediately before it turn right, down and through a newish kissing-gate. Cross the field almost diagonally and reach another, older, kissing-gate. In 20 more yards go over a wooden footbridge with handrails. Turn right and follow the stream on your right.

Ignore a wooden footbridge to your right but carry on to an iron skew footbridge, with handrail, which leads to the end of a road. Turn right along the road, past the bottle bank, to Market Street green, and at the end of it the White Horse pub again. On the green is the village sign, proclaiming 'Steadfast in Work and Play'.

10 Great Eversden
The Hoops

This is a farming area. From the twin villages of Great and Little Eversden, the land on the south-west side rises gradually to a rounded ridge about 200 ft above sea level, beyond which lies Wimpole Hall, its park and extensive farms. Almost at the crest of the hill is Eversden Wood, a large stand of mixed woodland. On a flat area about 2 miles to the east stand the dishes and masts of the Cambridge University Radio Astronomy Observatory.

The white-painted, grey-brown roofed pub has a happy atmosphere and every effort is made to make each customer feel at home. Swinging from a substantial pillar is the inn sign, showing a couple of children playing with their hoops. There are many innovative features at this well-run pub, including a monthly theme evening offering foods from round the world. The part of the pub nearest the road corner dates from the 19th century and the beams in the 17th-century restaurant were allegedly taken from 16th-century Spanish galleons. The public area is L-shaped, flowing round the corner from the restaurant, with only open stud-work subdividing the whole area. A huge log fire burns in the grate on chilly days.

A high proportion of the meals served are home-made. Steak and ale pie, chicken and vegetable pie, lasagne, pizzas, hash 'n' eggs, boeuf bourguignonne, mixed grill and chicken and Stilton roulades are firm favourites. Any of these dishes can be followed by apple crumble, treacle or jam sponge pudding, black cherry cheesecake or chocolate fudge cake. The real ales stocked are Charles Wells Eagle IPA, Marston's Pedigree and a guest, which is changed weekly. Strongbow draught cider is on offer as well. Children are made welcome. For a very modest sum a child can order a main course from a tempting menu, and will also have baked beans, a slice of bread and butter and a glass of squash or coke and an ice-cream. The play apparatus includes not one, but two superb Wendy houses, two climbing frames and more besides, in a large garden. There are changing facilities for small babies. In all a paradise for parents! Well-behaved dogs are allowed inside too. The pub is open both at lunchtime and in the evening every day of the week, and meals are served throughout opening times, except for Monday lunchtimes (only pizzas are served on Sunday and Monday evenings). Some overnight accommodation is also available.

Telephone: 01223 262185.

How to get there: Great Eversden is 5 miles west of Cambridge. Turn off the A603 some 3 miles south-west of junction 12 of the M11, following signs for Great and Little Eversden. The Hoops is about a mile from the A603.

Parking: Behind the pub is a large car park.

Length of the walk: 3 miles. OS map: Landranger sheet 154 Cambridge, Newmarket and surrounding area (inn GR 365535).

A pleasant walk over farmland. After passing the church, the route goes by a grassy footpath and lane past a vineyard to Merry's Farm. It continues up the hill on a cross-field footpath to Eversden Wood. A stroll through the wood leads to a headland path in a shallow valley and you return to the village on a sunken farm track past Manor Farm.

The Walk

From the pub go left towards the church, with its teeny spire atop its tower. Just before you reach it, turn right off the road into a broad, grassy area, and continue beside the ranch-style fence on the right. To the left the land rises to a ridge about a mile away.

Soon the fence ends and, on the right, a windbreak of Lombardy poplars and a hawthorn hedge protect a vineyard. At the corner, where the hawthorn hedge on the right ends, turn right into a little green lane, passing the vineyard on the right and hawthorns on the left. Keep on the narrow footpath, which leads shortly to Wimpole Road, and turn left.

In about 300 yards reach the farm buildings of Merry's Farm and, just after the last building on the right, turn right on a farm track with grass in the middle. After about 200 yards swing half-left on a well-walked path up the hill, keeping Great Eversden church tower directly in line behind you. When you reach a plateau keep straight on in the same direction, crossing a farm track en route. To your left you will see, 400 yards away, two low drum reservoirs.

As you approach Eversden Wood, initially head for a point halfway along its length, then, on getting nearer, you will see a hedge 50 yards in front of the wood. Go to the end of the hedge and drop down a little, over a culvert, and on towards the trees. Do not enter the wood, but go left on the broad green track just outside the tree line.

At the corner of the wood you meet an earth farm track. Go right along it, with the trees on your right. After about 200 yards, at a waymark, go right into the wood, firstly at a right angle, then almost immediately leftish. Keep straight on along the grassy track and do not take the left fork a bit later on. Quite soon look for another waymark, a three-way sign, about 2 yards off the path. Take this grassy drive to the right.

Come out of the wood at the corner of a vast field, with fine views. Ignore the path on your right, within the wood. Having left the trees, turn right and walk along the earth farm track, with an open field on your left. Pass through a cross-hedge and carry on till the woods on the right end, then swing left and walk down the valley, with a stream on your right.

Pass a culvert off to the right, and yet another where a track goes up to Merry's Farm on the right. When almost at the bottom

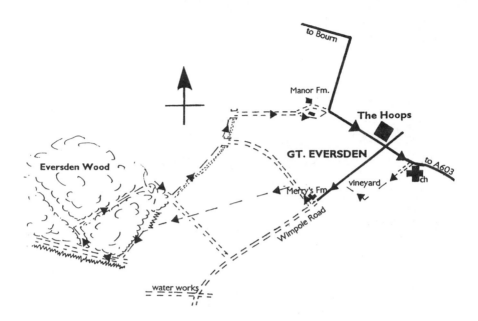

of the hill, at a waymark, you can see the village ahead about ½ mile away. Go right. Cross a culvert and then climb up, with a few trees each side and grass in the middle.

After the crest of this path you are in a sunken lane. Go on down to a metal farm gate. Presently the track swings left a little towards Manor Farm, and here you go rightish to pass to the right of the black weatherboarded barns, with a wire fence on your left. The route curves to the left, past a waymark, over a tiny footbridge and out to a two-step stile near the end of the farm drive, which is on your left.

Go on towards a large green metal farm gate and join the road. On your left you can see a gazebo and a Chinese bridge. Turn right along the road, with a wide verge on both sides, back to the Hoops.

Places of interest nearby
Wimpole Hall (National Trust) is in easy reach to the south-west. See pub walk 7 for details.

11 Colne
The Green Man

Colne, pronounced cone, is about a mile from the river Great Ouse, some 5 miles downstream of the town of St Ives. It is a fruit growing area and the village is encircled by orchards, perhaps because the land here is slightly higher than the surrounding fenland.

About 200 years ago this pub is reputed to have been the court room. It is also said to have a ghost. The old beams and the odd shaped doors suggest a long history. A big fireplace offers winter warmth, and the doors to the side lead to the garden, cool in the summer's heat. Blue upholstered benches are against all the walls – altogether a comfortable, relaxing inn.

A menu to make you feel hungry includes sizzling prawn Cantonese-style or teriyaki beef stir-fry, ham and mushroom tagliatelle, home-made steak pie, cheese-topped cottage pie, broccoli and cream cheese bake, chicken Kiev, moussaka and pepperoni and pasta bake. If you can find room for a dessert, you can choose from pineapple meringue and cream, chocolate fudge cake, 'Banana Shocker' and treacle sponge pudding. Burton Ale and Greene King IPA are on sale, and Dry Blackthorn draught cider. Children have their own menu and are made welcome. In the garden are a slide, a swing and a trapeze to amuse them. The pub is open, and serving food, every lunchtime and evening. Dogs may go inside, if well-behaved.

Telephone: 01487 840368.

How to get there: From all directions use the A1123 Huntingdon–St Ives–Ely road. At Earith, not far from the bridges over the Old and New Bedford rivers, turn north on the B1050 towards Somersham. In a mile, at a crossroads, turn left to reach the Green Man.

Parking: Beside the pub is a car park and there may be space for some roadside parking in the village side roads too.

Length of the walk: 4¼ miles, or 3 miles if you take the short-cut back along the road. OS map: Landranger sheet 142 Peterborough and surrounding area (inn GR 372758).

This delightful walk takes you as far as the village of Somersham and back, along field paths and beside orchards. A shorter route, returning by road from Somersham to Colne, is possible.

The Walk

From the Green Man go right along High Street and in 200 yards turn left down Old Church Lane. Keep on the lane as it bends sharp right in about a further 200 yards.

Where the lane bends left to Church Farm, leave it at a footpath sign and go along a concrete farm track towards a large, low barn, which you pass on the left. At a waymark at the end of the concrete, take a cross-field path towards a hedge corner. On the far side of the field continue in the same direction as before, through an orchard with a windbreak of poplars on the left. At the far corner turn right at the waymark, still following a line of poplars on the left. After about 70 yards, go left, again at a waymark, through a hedge and continue on a headland path, with a windbreak protecting an orchard on the right.

At the corner cross a sleeper bridge over a shallow ditch and turn left on a headland path with a ditch on the left. In about 100 yards turn right at a waymark in a corner by a few small trees, on a good cross-field path. Half-left you can see the tower of Somersham church. In the middle of the field, swing left, roughly towards the church, ignoring a track off to the right.

At a field corner cross a stile into a pasture and continue straight on, with a hedge and a fence on the left. Pass a cross-hedge and then some lagoons on the right, surrounded by chain link fencing. Cross a dilapidated stile and climb steps up a slight embankment to go over the former railway line, now a gravel track, and descend concrete steps on the other side to another stile. Continue, with a hedge and a ditch on the left.

On reaching the corner of the field, where a bridge leads straight on to the village of Somersham, turn right, with a ditch and a hedge on the left. Halfway along the ditch, at a waymark under an old willow tree, go half-right towards the corner of the field. Cross a stile into a wide, grassy way between hedges. Pass a small sawmill on the left and continue out to the road.

For the shorter walk, turn right along the road and in a mile turn right along High Street, back to the Green Man.

For the full walk, turn left along the road and very soon turn right at a T-junction on the B1050 towards Chatteris. Immediately bear left slightly and go up the station approach, over the former level crossing, where you can still see traces of the rails, then continue to join the main road once more.

Pass Bank Avenue on the left and stay on the Chatteris road, part of which is called The Bank. About $\frac{1}{2}$ mile from the former railway crossing, look out for a footpath sign and a long footbridge across the deep river on the right, opposite the entrance to 'Countryside Wild Flowers'. Cross the bridge and walk on a grassy area between a young mixed plantation of trees on the right and a ditch on the left.

At the end of the tree belt on the right, go left, crossing a footbridge over the ditch, and then turn right to follow, at first, a hedge and ditch on the right. Soon, keeping in the same direction, go alongside a field boundary with a few trees. Then walk beside a wire fence on the left, beyond which is a large gravel pit. There is a waymark on a corner fence post.

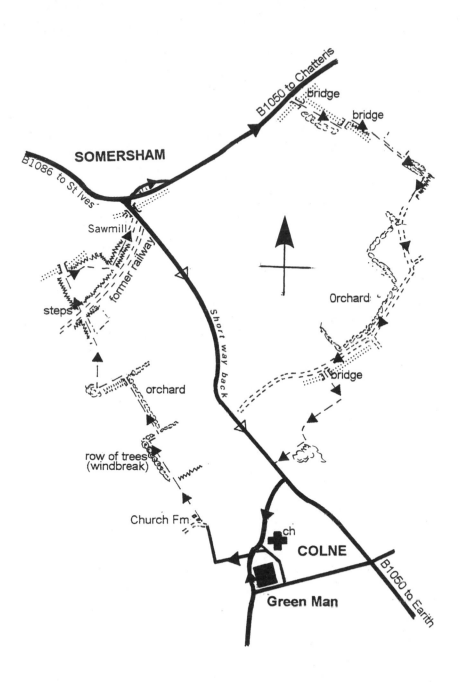

SOMERSHAM

B1086 to St Ives

B1050 to Chatteris

bridge

bridge

Sawmill

former railway

steps

Short way back

Orchard

bridge

orchard

row of trees
(windbreak)

Church Fm

ch

COLNE

B1050 to Earith

Green Man

Keep beside the wire fence until you reach some trees, then follow the waymark through them, along a narrow footpath. Eventually you can glimpse a lake beyond the trees on the left. Just as you reach the end of the tree belt swing right and pick up, at the corner of the field, a broad, grassy cart track with a hedge on the left.

Where the cart track sweeps round to the left, follow it and on the right, behind some trees, there is an orchard. Keep on this wide, grassy track as it veers round to the right and continue as it joins a gravelly, more heavily used, cart track which is coming in from the left. After about 100 yards there is a row of fruit trees on the right and soon a mature orchard.

Pass a track off to the left and continue on the gravel farm track, keeping the orchard on the right. When the orchard ends, stay on the track for just under 100 yards and turn left on a culvert, over the ditch on the left. Here, under a hawthorn tree, is a waymark. Walk away from the ditch on a narrow cross-field path along a crop division, and then, at another waymark, turn right along another crop division, which leads, in just under 100 yards, into a wide, grassy farm track.

The track bears slowly round to the left and when you reach the trees turn right and, following the trees on the left, continue on a cart track out to the road. Turn left and in 100 yards or so turn right along High Street. Pass the village green and, behind it, St Helen's church and in a few yards reach the Green Man.

Places of interest nearby
Approximately 5 miles away is the interesting town of *St Ives* with its ancient stone bridge, market place and museum. The *Norris Museum* situated by the side of the river is well worth a visit. Telephone 01480 465101 for details.

12 Great Chishill
The Pheasant

Great Chishill lies among gently rounded chalk hills in the southernmost part of Cambridgeshire, where it borders on Essex.

The Pheasant is a delightful, old world, 18th-century inn with timber beams. The L-shaped lounge-cum-restaurant has small tables dotted around, on each of which is a candle in a brass candlestick, and other brassware decorates the walls. A large garden up behind the pub is a pleasant place to eat when the weather allows.

The mouth-watering menu includes roast loin of pork, fillet of plaice in a dill sauce, poached salmon with prawn and basil sauce, rack of lamb, roast duck, marinated Orkney herrings and medallions of pork with a honey and mustard sauce. Game is available in season. To follow, you can choose from, for example, meringue and raspberry coulis, strawberry cheesecake, spotted dick and treacle sponge. All the food is freshly prepared on the premises. The Pheasant serves Ruddles Best, Directors and a weekly-changing guest ale, and Scrumpy Jack draught cider is also on offer. Children are welcome. There is a special menu for them and they will appreciate the garden, with its climbing net, tyre and ropes. The inn is open for drinking and eating each lunchtime and evening. On Saturday the hours are 'all day', from noon till 11 pm. Well-behaved dogs are allowed inside.

Telephone: 01763 838535.

How to get there: Great Chishill lies south of the A505 between junction 10 of the M11 and Royston. If travelling westwards, turn south onto a minor road signed to Heydon and Great Chishill. Bear right by Heydon church to reach the Pheasant in about a mile.

Parking: There is a car park at the rear of the pub. In addition, several parking spaces are located by the telephone box in the village.

Length of the walk: 3 miles (short-cuts possible). OS map: Landranger sheet 154 Cambridge, Newmarket and surrounding area (inn GR 423389).

This walk will be memorable for the extensive views from so many parts of the route as it circles the outside of the village envelope on high ground. After passing a fine postmill, you continue along headland paths and tracks and through an old quarry, now masked by a profusion of trees, shrubs and other vegetation.

The circuit could be shortened by omitting the path to the windmill and/or the northern loop through the quarry (see sketch map).

The Walk

From the Pheasant go left along the street for 100 yards or so to the red phone box. Turn left, up the steps, and climb up through the pleasant park. Pass through a wide gap into the next field and walk on up to the sports field. Go over the two-step stile and turn right alongside the paling fence. At the corner go left and join the road at the entrance drive to the sports field.

Turn right and walk down Hall Road, passing Waller's Grove and Colts Croft, and go left off the road beside No 30, just before

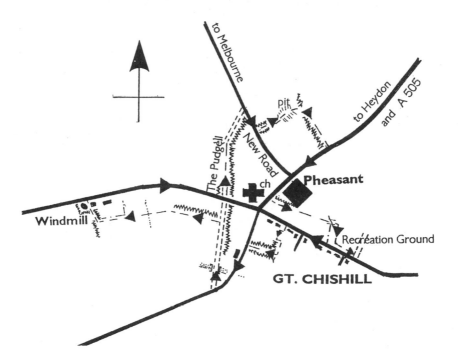

the thatched white house opposite. Follow the concrete track round the corner and by a street lamp go right, through a small wooden gate. The path snakes quite a bit until you emerge, over a bar, into the corner of a field which slopes away to the left, with fine views. Keep along the field edge, with the hedge on the right, and leave in the next corner, going right along a leafy lane until you meet the road, May Street.

Go left, passing thatched White Horse Cottage, and continue down the road. Near the bottom ignore a footpath that goes up some steps on the right. After passing May Street Farm swing sharply right off the road on a chalky field path, with a windmill seen in the distance away to the left.

Climb up on this grassy path, cross a stream, and when you pass the bank on the right a hedge begins. Keep beside the hedge until you reach the field corner. Turn left on a headland path, with the hedge on the right. There are wide views and you can see radio masts some 3 miles away. When the hedge ends keep on along a grass path into a slight valley, and stride a shallow ditch. At the corner of the field go right and walk out to the road beside the windmill. This was a fine postmill, built in 1819, using timber from a former windmill on the same site. It worked until 1951 and was restored in 1966.

Go right along the road back towards Chishill. (Alternatively, you could return the way you came and then turn left to rejoin the road.) When within sight of the church tower leave the road, going left into a lane called The Pudgell.

At the lane end, in a field corner, go downhill on a well-worn grass track, with a few trees on your right and extensive views. Bear round to the right with the path and climb the hill to join a road, by a metal barrier. Turn right and climb until you reach the 40 mph sign. About here leave the road, going left along a path with a cupressus hedge on the left. Emerge in the corner of a vast field, again with wide views. Continue down the hill, with a wire fence and hedge on the right.

Where the field edge swings left at the bottom you go right, through a gap, into a disused chalkpit. Follow the meandering path through it, with the land rising steeply to your right, until you come out at a T-junction of paths.

Turn right, at first with a ditch and an orchard beyond on the left, and then along a leafy glade. The path takes you out to the road in the village, opposite No 64. Turn right and walk back to the pub, passing New Road on your right.

Before you get there you will pass a small brick building on your left. It is about 10 ft by 10 ft and was the village lock-up, built sometime in the mid-1800s – there is a description for you to read. Not a very comfortable place for a felon to be confined!

Places of interest nearby
You can gain access to *Chishill windmill* between 1 April and 31 October by collecting the key from a nearby house.

13 Leverington
The Rising Sun

The village of Leverington is just a few miles from the town of Wisbech, which lies on the river Nene at the north-east corner of Cambridgeshire. This is a flat, low-lying area of rich, fertile farmland, criss-crossed with an intricate network of deep drainage ditches. Fruit is grown here and there are many orchards, protected by windbreaks of tall mature trees. Just south of the Rising Sun is Peppermint Hall and it has been suggested that peppermint was at one time a local crop in the area.

The cream-washed, broad-fronted Rising Sun, which is about 400 years old, has a friendly, welcoming atmosphere. The pub has two bars and there are sparkling horse brasses and a log fire for cooler days.

The menu is wide, with choices for meat eaters, vegetarians and fish lovers. Steak, lamb cutlets, plaice, sole and cod, delicious spicy chicken, pork chops and chicken curry are among the dishes offered. A range of sweets, such as apple pie, spotted dick, treacle pudding, Alabama fudge cake and lemon cheesecake, is also there for the ordering. The real ales are from the Elgood's brewery, which is but a short distance away, on the North Brink in Wisbech. Strongbow draught cider is available too. Children seated with their parents for a meal are welcome. They have a special menu, and the garden is there for them to play in. The Rising Sun is open all the normal hours, and meals are served at lunchtime and in the evening throughout the week.

Telephone: 01945 583754.

How to get there: Leverington lies north-west of Wisbech. Travelling on the A1101 between Wisbech and Tydd Gote, turn off westwards on the B1169, north of the river Nene. The Rising Sun is a further 1/2 mile, at a junction where the main road bends sharp left.

Parking: The pub's car park is quite large.

Length of the walk: 4 miles, or 1³/₄ miles if you take the short-cut. OS map: Landranger sheet 143 Ely, Wisbech and surrounding area (inn GR 445108).

The walk, on the north-western side of Wisbech, is, for the most part, on well-frequented paths and quiet village roads with views out over the flat fenland plain. For a short distance the route follows Sea Bank, sometimes called Roman Bank, an earth embankment some 2 metres high, no doubt a former protection against flooding from the tidal river Nene.

The Walk

From the Rising Sun go straight over the road and follow the B1169 towards Leverington Common. Keep on the footway, passing an attractive old barn on the right. Turn right at the next corner, by Three Ways Farm with its collection of old farm implements, into Ringers Lane.

Some 100 yards after passing the end of Knights Close, turn right by the Six Ringers public house and walk along Gorefield Road towards St Leonard's church. Note the four unusual round turrets above the tower parapet, beside the spire. Take the tarmac path within the churchyard wall, pass the south porch and leave the churchyard at the corner by the T-junction.

Cross over the road to Newton and take the signed footpath

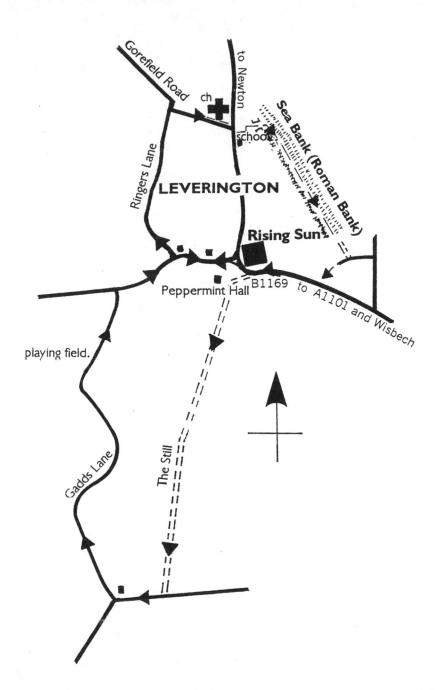

Gorefield Road

to Newton

ch

Sea Bank (Roman Bank)

Ringers Lane

school

LEVERINGTON

Rising Sun

Peppermint Hall

B1169 to A1101 and Wisbech

playing field.

Gadds Lane

The Still

immediately to the left of the school. Zigzag left then right round the school playing field, on the path between fences. Cross a long wooden footbridge and turn right. You are now beside Sea Bank (Roman Bank), covered with trees and bushes, on the left and a ditch on the right.

Continue on this pleasant grass path beside the high bank for more than ¼ mile. Take the opportunities provided by tracks between bushes to climb the bank here and there. Eventually the grass gives way to a tarmac drive which leads you out to a narrow road, where you turn right. The road becomes progressively narrower and is blocked, at its end, by bollards.

Cross a ditch and turn right along the footway beside the B1169 road, passing a seat. The road, with a deep ditch on the right, bends slowly left. Opposite, on the left, is a house with a green telephone box in its garden.

For the shorter walk, keep along this road and you will reach the Rising Sun in about 200 yards.

For the full walk, cross the B1169, where it bends sharply round to the right, and go straight on between white gateposts, along a narrow tarmac road known as The Still. In a few yards, within sight of Peppermint Hall, keep left along the tarmac lane, following a brick wall on the left for about 100 yards, after which you come out to open fields. The octagonal building away to the left is the remains of a former dog pound.

Keep on the hard cart track, crossing several deep drainage ditches. The view around is of the rich, intensively cultivated agricultural land.

The Still eventually comes out to Barton Road, where you turn right. Just as the road bends sharply left you turn right into Gadds Lane, a quiet road. Continue, passing a number of orchards, for about a mile. Towards the end is Leverington Playing Field, given to the village by George Munday MC who lived at Leverington Hall, close by the church from 1936 to 1967.

At the T-junction at the end turn right and in 250 yards pass, on the left, Ringers Lane, where you walked earlier, and continue along the road back to the Rising Sun.

Places of interest nearby
The charming old market town of *Wisbech* is within easy reach of Leverington.

14 Witcham
The White Horse Inn

Witcham is a small, isolated fenland village not far from Ely. Settlements in this area tended to be wherever the land was slightly higher, and Witcham is on a small hill about 50 ft above the fens. The lanes are generally wide, perhaps because the land is soft and a single width cart track would get too rutted.

The White Horse pub has several distinct areas, including a restaurant down a couple of steps from another comfortable seating area, resplendent with easy chairs as well as tables. Then on the other side of the bar and entrance is a bistro, with wheelback chairs and its own serving facilities. Soft music plays as you dine.

Spicy chicken, ham and bacon pasta, chicken curry, vegetable curry, Cajun chicken, Polynesian chicken and gammon steaks are just a few of the main courses available in the bar. Among the sweets are crêpes, profiteroles, sticky toffee pudding, butterscotch surprise and Caribbean sundae. The restaurant is mainly for evening meals when there is an extended menu. There are occasional special food evenings, for which booking is essential.

The real ales available are Greene King IPA, Nethergate, Bodding-tons and a changing guest. Stowford Press draught cider is on sale too.

The pub is open at lunchtime and in the evening from Tuesday to Sunday. Food is served throughout opening times, except on Sunday evenings. Well-behaved dogs may go into the bar.

Telephone: 01353 778298.

How to get there: Witcham lies north of the A142 between Ely and Chatteris. Turn off the main road 4 miles west of Ely. In the village turn left along Silver Street to the White Horse.

Parking: The pub has its own car park.

Length of the walk: 2³/₄ miles OS Map: Landranger sheet 143 Ely, Wisbech and surrounding area (inn GR 462799).

This is a pleasant and easy walk, at first along Wardy Hill Road, a broad, grassy, hedge-lined track which leads towards Wardy Hill, a tiny settlement on a small hill rising about 30 ft above the surrounding fens. Before reaching Wardy Hill, the lane crosses a broad drainage watercourse expressively called the Catchwater Drain. The walk then continues beside the drain and returns along a leafy, narrow footpath, back to Witcham.

The Walk

From the White Horse turn right along Silver Street and go straight over the crossroads into High Street, passing the village recreation ground on the left. Some 15 yards or so beyond St Martin's church turn left at a footpath sign and walk between a brick wall on the left and a wire fence, which soon becomes a wooden ranch-style fence, on the right. At the end of the paddock on the right, cross a two-sleeper footbridge over a ditch and continue straight on for about 15 yards with a hedge on the left, out to a lane. Turn right.

In 40 yards turn left onto Wardy Hill Road. This is signed 'Public Byway' and is a broad earth track running between wide-spaced hedges. Pass an isolated cottage on the left.

After about ¹/₄ mile along this lane the hedges on both sides are cut lower and there are excellent views in all directions. You are

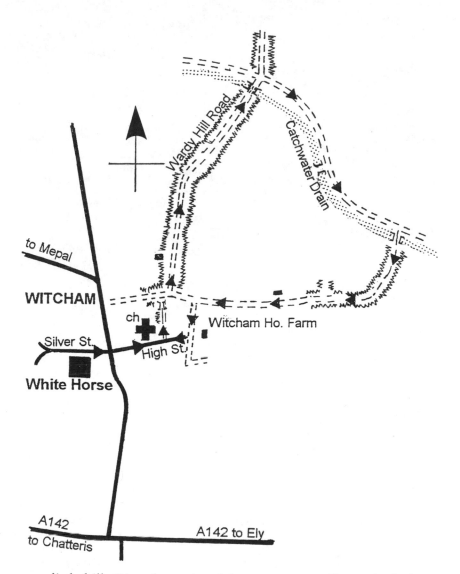

on a little hill. Directly to the right you can see Ely Cathedral. In front, a few fields away, is the small rise of Wardy Hill.

Descend slightly to a point where the broad, grassy track narrows to cross a culvert over the Catchwater Drain, beyond which the path you are on crosses another track. Here turn right and walk along a track on a low bank, beside the Catchwater

The view along Green Lane.

Drain on the right, and 20 yards away on the left is another ditch. In about ¼ mile the track widens out for a short distance and there are gates on both sides, but keep straight on beside the wide ditch on the right.

At a T-junction of tracks turn right and immediately cross the Catchwater Drain by a wide culvert into a lane called Bury Road, which is rather different from the tracks used previously. It is a narrow, grassy path between tall hedges, which after several minor twists bends round to the right and gets slightly wider.

The lane eventually comes out to a more heavily used, rutted track. Pass on the right a grassy lane between hedges and, when the track becomes wider, pass a white house called 'The Brickyard' on the right. Soon come to a bungalow, also on the right, and brick and tiled barns. Here you are just within sight of the end of Wardy Hill Road where you were earlier. Turn left at a T-junction, along a pot-holey tarmac road.

After going past the entrance to Witcham House Farm, on the left, turn right into High Street, just by the entrance to Victorian Witcham House. Walk straight down High Street, passing the church, and return to the White Horse.

15 Fen Ditton
The Ancient Shepherds

The pretty village of Fen Ditton lies on the north-eastern edge of the city of Cambridge, bounded near its northern side by the A14 road and on its western side by the river Cam. Eights, fours and skiffs train on the tranquil river, under the drooping willows. The monks of Ely held large estates in the area, some of which were given to them by King Canute. The walk passes close to Biggin Abbey, which is now a farmhouse, but is said to have been the seat of the Bishops of Ely.

The Ancient Shepherds, which stands in the High Street, is a welcoming pub. It is also quiet – no darts, no pool and no juke box. The building has been there since about 1540 and the whole place exudes atmosphere.

Some of the dishes offered are steak and kidney pie, cold roast beef, ham and chips, rack of lamb, pork stroganoff and nut Wellington. Among the tempting desserts are treacle sponge, banana pancakes with home-made butterscotch sauce, profiteroles and lemon brûlée. A non-smoking restaurant will please many.

Tolly, Tetley and Flowers ales are stocked, and Blackthorn Dry cider. Children are welcome, and there is a garden area for them to romp in outside. The pub is open at all the usual hours and meals are served throughout the week, except on Sunday evenings.

Telephone: 01223 293280.

How to get there: From the north and west, use the A14 and peel off at the slip road for the B1047, signed 'Cambridge'. Turn right and in a mile turn right again. The Ancient Shepherds is a few hundred yards away on the left. From the east, leave the A14 at the interchange for Cambridge (A1303). In ½ mile go right for Fen Ditton. At the crossroads keep straight on.

Parking: Plenty of parking space is available at the rear of the pub. There is also street-side parking in the village.

Length of the walk: 3 miles. OS map: Landranger sheet 154 Cambridge, Newmarket and surrounding area (inn GR 485602).

Starting along Fen Ditton's interesting main street, the route runs alongside the river for a while, then turns away and crosses farm paths past Biggin Abbey, going over to Baits Bite Lock and back alongside the river, to the gentle accompaniment of synchronised blades entering the water at intervals as the occasional college boat goes by.

The Walk

Turn left and walk down the High Street, passing some attractive houses, as far as the church. Turn right and walk along winding Church Street, passing Willy's Almshouses and an old black and white house with a jettied upper storey, to the road's end, by some bungalows facing across the water meadows to the river.

Keep straight on, going through a kissing-gate, across a meadow and, passing to the right of an isolated farm cottage and then to the right of a pylon, out by a two-step stile. Turn left and then swing right under the A14 road, where it crosses the river by a massive bridge. Now immediately go right over a two-step stile along a footpath which is going towards Horningsea. Follow the path beside the main road fence to a point under a pylon, and turn left on a well-marked cross-field path.

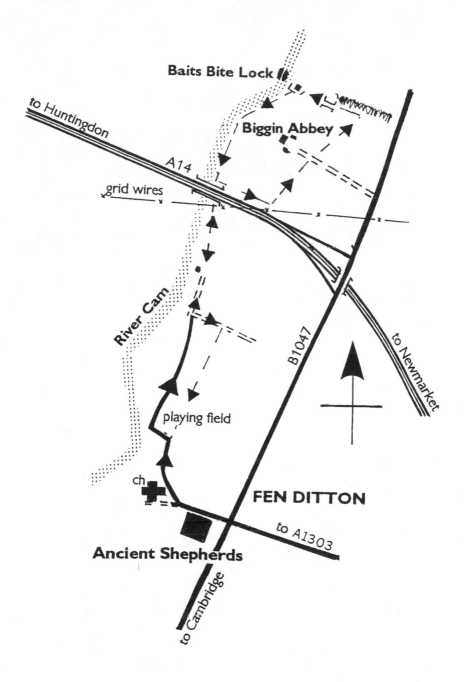

Baits Bite Lock

Biggin Abbey

to Huntingdon

A14

grid wires

River Cam

playing field

B1047

to Newmarket

ch

FEN DITTON

to A1303

Ancient Shepherds

to Cambridge

The weir near Bait Bite Lock.

Go over a farm drive which leads to Biggin Abbey on your left, looking for all the world like the farmhouse it is. Continue across the next field to meet a ditch and a hedge. Turn left, now on the Harcamlow Way, crossing a small wooden footbridge and on, bearing slightly leftish by the white house on your right. When you reach a fence ahead, make a short detour by going to the right to visit pretty Baits Bite Lock.

Now return and go through the metal kissing-gate, keeping the high wood fence on your right for a bit, then continuing beside the river. After going under the A14 again, cross a two-step stile into the meadow you were in earlier. Walk over it to pass the lonely cottage on your right and retrace your steps to the end of the road you walked along earlier.

Do not follow the road, but turn left from the cul-de-sac end, along the Fen River Way on a stony track between hedges. In 200 yards go right at a footpath sign, on a well-used headland path. Pass through a gap and enter the playing field. Carry straight on, passing a brick pavilion, and emerge at the far side into Church Street, and so return to the pub.

16 Hinxton
The Red Lion

Hinxton and Ickleton are a pair of small villages lying in the valley of the Cam, on the southern edge of Cambridgeshire. Although a mere 8 miles from the city of Cambridge, and close to the National Air Museum and airfield of Duxford, with a nearby industrial estate, the area is very quiet, having been bypassed by the A1301 and the M11.

The Red Lion is a romantic 16th-century coaching inn that has been sensitively extended and subtly subdivided into many small, intimate areas. Deep inside it an old bread oven has been discovered. The theme of the pub is natural history and a great array of animals, birds and fishes, some as wood carvings, some in brass, some as ceramic models and some stuffed, in glass cases, are around the walls, beams and fireplace. George the parrot, definitely live, has pride of place in the bar area, while a stuffed tarantula spider adorns the porch wall. In the grounds are more livestock – Anna the pony and Posey the goat.

The menu is broad, and vegetarians are well catered for.

Something is sure to please – you will find home-baked ham, lasagne, hot smoked mackerel, salmon and broccoli quiche, spicy cottage pie and asparagus quiche, among other dishes, then lattice apple tart, treacle sponge, spotted dick, toffee meringue gateau and much, much more. The real ales served are Greene King IPA, Adnams, Bass and Boddingtons. Dry Blackthorn draught cider is also sold. Well-behaved children dining with their parents are welcome. The pub is open at the usual hours and meals are served both at lunchtime and in the evening. Dogs are not allowed inside.

Telephone: 01799 530601.

How to get there: From Cambridge you could take the M11 south, exit at Duxford (junction 10) onto the A505 eastwards and in 2 miles, at a roundabout, go south on the A1301 for 1½ miles to the turn off for Hinxton. From other directions, make your way to Stump Cross, a major roundabout where the A11 joins the M11 and the A1301. Go north along the A1301 for 1 mile before turning off to Hinxton. The Red Lion is near the church.

Parking: Behind the pub is a large car park. There is also a little on-street parking.

Length of the walk: 3¼ miles. OS map: Landranger sheet 154 Cambridge, Newmarket and surrounding area (inn GR 496451).

The terrain is rolling farmland with a good sprinkling of small woods, making for pleasant walking. The route goes, beside the Cam at times, to the nearby village of Ickleton. The circuit is almost entirely on field paths and green lanes.

The Walk

From the Red Lion go right, passing Church Green, a few thatched houses and some half-timbered dwellings with jettied upper storeys. Turn left into Mill Lane and at a bend go left along a fenced path to Hinxton water mill, a 17th-century timber-framed corn mill, adjoining a mid-19th-century miller's cottage. It was restored to working order in 1986 by the Cambridge Preservation Society.

Snake right round the mill and cross over the sluice. Go right,

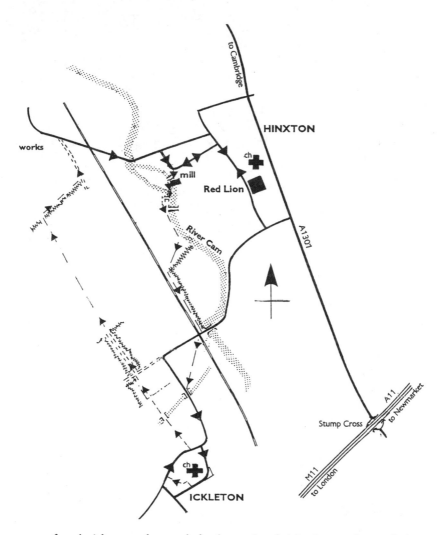

over a footbridge, and turn left along the field edge and parallel to the river until you reach a field corner, where you join a riverside path. Nearby, you will see a private bridge over the river. Keep beside the river Cam, on the left, as it bends. Shortly bear right, away from the river, beside a hedge on the left, to the field corner. Go left through a gap beside a farm gate, with the railway now on your right. Continue to the track's end, where you join a road.

Turn right along the road and with care go over the level

crossing. Immediately leave the road again, going left over a stile. Cross the field diagonally to the red-brick wall seen at the far side, well to the right of the church spire. Leave by a stile and go left along the road. At a road junction go left into Church Street, past the leaning flint churchyard wall, propped up with brick buttresses, to the small green where you can rest on the seats around the chestnut tree opposite the church.

Pass the house with two dark red gables and turn right up the wide, funnelled path towards some metal gates. Beside the gates turn left into a narrow snicket, which curves up to meet another village road.

Go right along the road, with a high flint wall on your left. Just before the wall ends there is a gap. Go through it, over the stile, into a sunken lane. At the end leave by a stile to enter a long, narrow field. At the far left corner go over or through some rails and cross a two-sleeper footbridge into a large L-shaped field. Go straight ahead towards an internal corner of the field, roughly following electricity wires, and go over a high one-step stile. Keep beside the wire fence to the far end of the field, and leave by the stile there.

Turn right for 3 yards and then left into a green lane. Climb quite steeply and emerge from the lane to a plateau with wide views. Hinxton is on your right beyond the shallow valley of the Cam.

Continue in the same direction as before, now following the three electricity wires across the field. When they eventually go right you carry straight on for several more hundred yards to cross a stile in a hedge, by a three-way footpath sign. Turn right, with the hedge on the right until it ends, when you swing left on a raised grassy bank all the way out to join a road by a stile beside big white metal gates.

Turn right along the road and go over the level crossing. Cross a footbridge beside a ford through the river Cam, then turn into a road on the right. Follow the road round past the water mill and retrace your steps back into Hinxton.

Places of interest nearby
Duxford, the vast aircraft wing of the Imperial War Museum, is about a mile away, to the north-west. It is open every day of the year, except 24, 25 and 26 December. Telephone: 01223 835000.

17 Ely
The Cutter Inn

This delightful cathedral city, set on a hill in the otherwise flat fenland, is well worth a visit and there is much to see. The Cathedral of the Fens, commenced in 1081, is built within the walls of a very large Benedictine monastery. Its beautiful, soaring, octagonal tower is breathtaking and below the west tower there is a floor maze. Several imposing buildings of the former monastery can still be seen and the 15th-century Bishop's Palace stands beside the green alongside the magnificent west front of the cathedral.

The Cutter Inn was originally a brewery and maltings, as early as 1679, and Cutter Lane was known as Beer Lane. It has been a pub since the 1830s. The large, cream-washed building has two bars, both having river views. Just outside, and only feet from the river, are lots of tables and benches for alfresco meals and drinking on hot days. There are bar games in the larger of the bars.

Sirloin, fillet and gammon steaks, pork chops, beef and Guinness pie, chicken Kiev, chicken and mushroom pie, the Cutter mixed grill and lasagne are some of the dishes on offer, as are gateau and cream, cheesecake, chocolate nut sundae, banana split and apple pie. The real ales stocked are Ruddles County, Ruddles Best, Webster's Yorkshire Bitter and Adnams. Scrumpy Jack and Strongbow draught cider are also on sale. Children are welcome, and they have their own menu – beefburgers, fish fingers, sausages and eggs with chips. As the water is only yards from the inn, they will, of course, need supervision. The inn is open all day, every day and meals are served at lunchtime and in the evening throughout the week. Well-behaved dogs are allowed inside.

Telephone: 01353 662713.

How to get there: From Cambridge, the north and the west, use the Ely bypass (the A10) and take the A142 towards Newmarket. At a roundabout just south of Ely, where the A142 goes right to cross the railway 200 yards away, take the first exit (left), towards the town centre. Almost immediately, and before a triangular tree-lined verge on the right, go sharp right into Annesdale. This road leads to the river, just by the Cutter. From the Newmarket direction, cross the railway and keep straight on (second exit) at the roundabout. Then go sharp right.

Parking: Behind the inn is a large car park, and there are also a few places on the riverside. There is a large public car park in the city, within easy reach of the Cutter.

Length of the walk: 2¹/₂ miles. OS map: Landranger sheet 143 Ely, Wisbech and surrounding area (inn GR 544797).

This walk follows the western bank of the north-flowing river Great Ouse, swings west by Roswell Pits and continues to the Market Place by way of Springhead Lane. You get an opportunity to stroll through the cathedral precincts before returning to the Cutter Inn, down on the waterfront once more.

The Walk
From the Cutter Inn go left alongside the river, passing the boathouse of King's School Boat Club on the opposite bank. Pass Ely Maltings and soon come to a long brownish brick building with a red-tiled roof, cream windows, and a lucam halfway along the roofline.

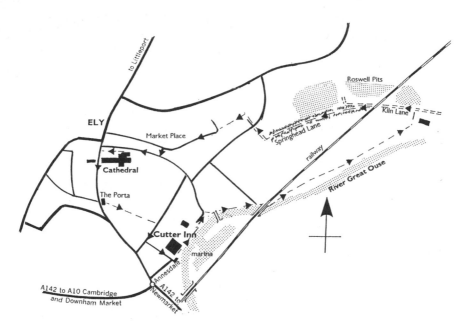

Swing right, with the long building on your left, and walk to the left of the private bridge, going down a concrete ramp. This leads to a quiet, grassy area with seats and beautiful willow trees.

Join a road at its end, where it bends. Go right on a narrow riverside footpath, under the railway bridge, through a wooden pedestrian gate, and carry on along the river bank, awash in season with a sea of buttercups. Further on, where there are water-filled lagoons on the left, bear away a little from the river's edge, going up a slight bank. Look back at the fine view of the cathedral. There is now a tall hawthorn hedge on your left. You may hear geese honking away on the washlands.

When the riverside path comes to an end by some grey industrial buildings, go out through a long kissing-gate, big enough for wheelchairs to negotiate, and turn left, on Ely's Easy Access Trail.

Follow the path up past the car park, and join a quiet road and turn left. You will see the symbol of the Hereward Way on a post hereabouts. With care, go over the Kiln Lane railway crossing with its automatic barriers.

Almost immediately swing left, off the road, into Springhead Lane. Take time to read the information board about the area.

The fact that where now there are **pits** was once known as Roswell **Hill** tells a story about the vast amounts of clay that have been removed.

Follow this green lane through the wooded area until you have just passed a wooden footbridge and steps on your left. Now your path begins to curve round to the right and you soon go out through a wooden barrier to a road. Cross straight over, still on the Hereward Way, under a big horse chestnut tree and climb up beside bungalows. Meet a cul-de-sac estate road and go left, keeping up above the bungalows, on a narrow path. At the end go right on a tiny cul-de-sac called Vineyard Way and very soon turn left into The Vineyards, with the cathedral ahead of you.

Towards the end of this narrow road follow it round to the right and into the Market Place. Cross diagonally towards the end of the High Street and go through the broad arch, the Sacrist's Gate, in the wall which surrounds the cathedral, into the precincts. Go right and walk towards the west end.

Turn left across the great west entrance to the cathedral, and proceed to the left of the old Bishop's Palace, now a Sue Ryder Home. Walk along The Gallery as far as a small green, Barton Square, and an impressive gateway on the left, known as the Porta, or Walpole's Gate.

Pass under the Porta, at one time a gate of the abbey, and go straight ahead to the park. Follow the tarmac path all the way down the hill and leave by the gates at the bottom. Turn right for a block or so and then go left into Victoria Street, at the bottom of which you bear left beside the river, back to the Cutter.

Places of interest nearby

High inside the cathedral is the *Stained Glass Museum*, open from May through to October. Besides its own interesting exhibits, it offers sweeping views down into the nave. There is also a *Brass Rubbing Centre* in the cathedral. For bookings, telephone 01353 667735. *Cromwell's House* stands at the end of the green, not far from the west front of the cathedral. It was his home for 10 years and is open to the public.

18 Soham
The Cherry Tree

Soham is a market town with a busy industrial area, about 5 miles north-west of Newmarket, and close to the Suffolk border. The country to the south and east is rolling and well-peppered with trees and hedges. To the west and north, however, are the Cambridgeshire Fens, a flat, wet plain of rich, black, peaty soil stretching to Ely and beyond. A river, called the Soham Lode, flows through the town to join the river Great Ouse just south of Ely.

The Cherry Tree is a delightful hostelry on the southern edge of the town. The two bars are not quite separate, divided only by a wall partway across the large room. The end wall is glazed wall-to-wall, giving good views of the bandstand, garden and well-equipped play area. There can be few other pubs which have a full-sized bandstand in their garden – brass bands play here on summer Sunday evenings, a very pleasant listening experience. A welcoming atmosphere awaits you and nothing seems to be too much trouble. The doors from the lounge bar lead out onto a patio with more tables and chairs, and summertime sunshades.

The wide range of food includes roast chicken, beef and lamb, gammon steak, pizza, home-made shepherd's pie, lasagne and Chinese spring rolls. To follow there are some very tempting desserts, such as apple pie, mincemeat slice, cherry pie, apple strudel and bread and butter pudding. Greene King ales are available and Dry Blackthorn draught cider is on sale too. Children are well catered for, with plenty of play apparatus in the very large garden and their own menu. The pub is open each lunchtime and evening, and all day on Saturday. Meals are available at each session, apart from Sunday evenings. Dogs are welcome, if well-behaved.

Telephone: 01353 720405.

How to get there: Soham is just off the A142 Newmarket to Ely road. Go to the roundabout, just south of Soham, where the A142 meets the A1123 to Stretham. Take the local road to Soham. The Cherry Tree is about ½ mile from the roundabout.

Parking: There is a wide space for lots of cars in front of the pub.

Length of the walk: 3 miles. OS map: Landranger sheet 154 Cambridge, Newmarket and surrounding area (inn GR 603721).

This walk is mostly along green lanes and well-used footpaths. It starts across farmland at the edge of the town and, after crossing the bypass, reaches the bank of the Soham Lode. The route follows the river to the town centre. The return is through the grounds of the Soham Village College and across an area called The Butts (perhaps where, in Tudor times, yeomen of the town practised their archery), then along Cherrytree Lane, back to the start.

The Walk

From the Cherry Tree go right along the road away from Soham. Cross the road and, in about 150 yards, pass a road off to the right. A few yards further, after a pair of houses on the left, go left at a 'Public Byway' sign, along a cart track with, at first, hedges both sides. Very shortly the hedges give way to open fields, left and right. Soon, away to the right, you can see a

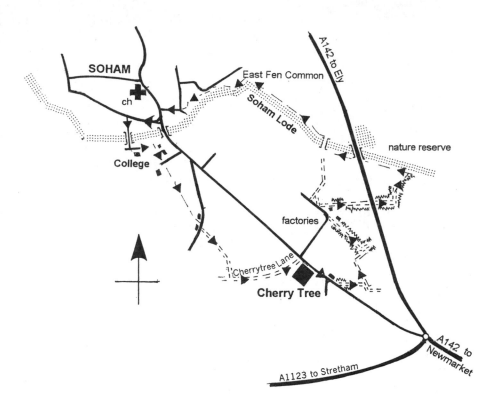

windmill, and half-right a typically Victorian water tower with a pyramidal roof.

At a waymark, where the cart track goes right for a few yards, turn left away from the track along a headland path with a ranch-style fence on the right. At the field end follow the fence round to the right for about 25 yards to meet a leafy lane at a corner. Turn left and walk along this green lane, crossing straight over a pair of stiles beside steel gates. After passing a bungalow on the right, come out to a road at a right-angled corner.

Go straight on to Greenhill, the first turning on the right. Bear right into the entrance to Greenhill but immediately go right along a lane off to the right, beside a weatherboarded fence. Pass a bungalow on the right and continue on this cart track, with a hedge on the left and, eventually, a hedge on the right.

Carefully cross the Soham bypass and continue on the byway, with hedges both sides. Keep on the lane as it turns sharp left.

Cross a stile beside a gate at the end of the byway and continue along the green lane to reach the edge of the wide watercourse known as Soham Lode.

Go left along the river bank, with the river on your right. On the opposite side of the water is the Soham Meadows Nature Reserve.

At the main road cross a stile, carefully go over the carriageways, cross another stile on the opposite side and continue beside the Lode on your right. Follow the river to reach a footbridge, then turn right across it and go left along the river bank. At the end of the field go over a stile. Soham church tower can be seen, half-left. Continue beside the Lode on the left, through East Fen Common with its old willow trees.

Where the river makes a right-angled turn to the left, continue along the bank beside the Lode. Shortly bear slightly away from the river and walk on a narrow path, beside some garden fences, which comes out beside a road. Almost immediately, where the road bends right, continue on a tarmac path veering away to the left. In about 200 yards the path leads out to a road at a bend.

At this point, if you look sharp-left, you can see the Lode and there is a grassed area and a few seats beside it.

Go roughly straight on along the road, that is, in the same direction as you were walking on the tarmac footpath, to Soham town centre. At the T-junction, opposite the Red Lion, turn left for 20 yards and then turn right at the war memorial. Pass the library on the left, and then turn left along College Road. Pass Lode Close on the right, cross a river bridge into the grounds of Soham Village College and turn left along a car park beside the Lode on the left.

At the end of the car park there is a road going straight ahead to a sports centre, but here, at a footpath signed 'Public Footpath The Butts ½', turn right on the wide concrete track with a hedge on the left. Go straight through the college grounds, passing a sports hall and various educational buildings on the left. Continue in the same direction and, after passing another small car park and tennis courts away to the right, cross a road giving access to the primary school.

At this point, leaving the tarmac, continue on a narrow gravel path, with a hedge on the left and a fenced playing field on the right. At the end of the playing field go over a stile and continue,

The Soham Lode river.

still with a hedge on the left and a fence on the right. The path you are on eventually swings left out to a road between houses.

At the road go a few yards to the right and continue on a cart track in the same direction as before, now with hedge on the right and allotments on the left.

A few yards after leaving the allotments you reach a T-junction of tracks. Go left along Cherrytree Lane, a green lane with hedges both sides. The prominent squarish building which can be seen to the left is a plastics factory. The lane leads back to the Cherry Tree.

Places of interest nearby

Soham Meadows, a Wildlife Trust nature reserve and one of the most important areas of grassland remaining in Cambridgeshire. An information board explains that these meadows are a remnant of the damp pasture that was once common in fenland. They have provided summer pasturage at least since the Middle Ages and grazing is still regulated by the Fen Reeves on behalf of the Lord of the Manor. The hedges skirting the meadow, interesting wildlife habitats, date back to Anglo Saxon times.

19 Horseheath
The Old Red Lion

Horseheath lies on the south-eastern side of Cambridgeshire, close to the Suffolk border and surrounded by rolling farmland.

The Old Red Lion is at the most westerly point in the village, on high ground with distant views. An 18th-century inn, it has some flagstone floors and timber beams. It also offers overnight accommodation, giving you an opportunity to explore the area further. The public area comprises the fairly new, large restaurant at the rear of the premises, up a step from the older bar area. The bar itself is subtly subdivided by small walls. On the grass to the front and side of the pub are a number of tables and benches for warmer days.

On the bar menu are sirloin steak, Cumberland sausage, steak and kidney pudding, hotpot, smoked trout, salmon steak and jacket potatoes with a choice of five fillings. Then you can select from fruits of the forest cheesecake, cherry pie, pineapple fritters and some wonderful old-fashioned puddings. In the evenings the large restaurant is open and offers another menu. Several times a month special culinary events are organised, such as 'A Taste of the Orient', 'A Taste of Portugal', 'A Taste of Greece' and 'Billy Bunter's Gutbuster Night'. For these evenings booking is recommended. Ales on offer are Ruddles Best, County and John Smith's, as well as a guest beer which changes every week. Children are welcome here and a special menu is supplied for them. All the usual hours are kept and on Saturdays the pub stays open all day. Dogs are not allowed inside.

Telephone: 01223 892909

How to get there: Horseheath is just off the A604 Cambridge to Colchester road and is about 4 miles west of Haverhill. The Old Red Lion is at the western end of the village, on the spur from the A604.

Parking: The pub car park is large. There is also some on-street parking in the village.

Length of the walk: 3 miles. OS map: Landranger sheet 154 Cambridge, Newmarket and surrounding area (inn GR 609472).

An exhilarating walk with many good views. From the centre of the village the route follows a headland path beside a stream through a shallow valley towards Streetly Hall, a prominent building on a small hill. The walk continues for a mile along an ancient track, part of the Roman road which ran from Durolipons (Cambridge) to a settlement near Horseheath. The return is along farm tracks and cross-field paths to the church.

The Walk
From the pub go right, swinging left at the small triangular green, and when opposite Cornish Close leave the road, going into a narrow path, signed 'To Streetly Hall ¾ mile', between fences. Shortly come out to a grassy area at the rear of some bungalows. Cross the grass and go rightish by an electricity pole to climb over a stile into a meadow.

Follow the fence on the right to the far end, go into the next field and near the end go right over a stile, through a hawthorn hedge and immediately turn left. For about 20 yards walk between the hedge on the left and a deep ditch on your right, then continue

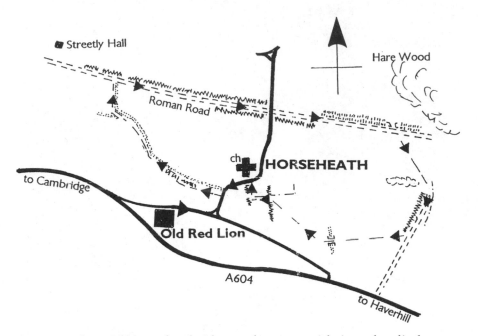

over a three-sleeper footbridge and go on with just the ditch on the right for about ½ mile.

At the far corner of the big field, before a wide metal gate, go right across the stream and climb the hill along the old Roman road, a broad grassy track with a hedge on the left. As you climb you will see the white Old Red Lion away to the south, at the edge of the village. A windmill at Streetly End can be seen to the north.

When you meet a cross-hedge to your right carry straight on, now in a green lane. A cross-path intersects your route here, indicated by the stiles on either side. Leave the green lane by a gap in the wooden rail fence, go out to the road and cross straight over. Go ahead along a farm track, with a ditch and a hedge on the right. This is an old Roman road.

Keep straight on when a deep ditch commences on your left. Presently, by a long gap in the hedge on your left, there is a wooden footbridge on the left, with a handrail. At this point you leave the track you have been on and swing right on a field path, walking towards the point where a wooden fence away on the left gives way to a hedge.

90

View from the old Roman road.

On the left are some Cedars of Lebanon. At the end keep on, with a fence on the left and a hedge on the right. The broad grass path swings slowly to the right and the ditch changes sides, from right to left now. When the hedge on the right ends, electricity wires are seen overhead. Turn right and follow under the wires that go across the field to the right, on the marked path.

Later go ahead to cross a stream by a wooden footbridge with handrails. Continue in the same direction for another 120 yards and then turn right across the field, heading for the left end of the ranch-style fence, seen roughly to the left of the church.

Go through a gap in the tall hedge to the left of the fence, and follow a grass path with a wire fence on your left until you are confronted by a high cupressus hedge. Do not go over the stile in the gap, but turn right and follow the path out by a stile to the road, opposite the church. Turn left along the village street, round to the right by the green, and back to the pub.

Places of interest nearby
The small hamlet of *Streetly End*, just north of Horseheath, has many thatched cottages and is a delight to see.

20 Kirtling
The Queen's Head

At the eastern edge of Cambridgeshire, about 5 miles south of Newmarket, Kirtling lies in a landscape of gently undulating hills and valleys, covered in a mixture of cultivated fields and pastures interspersed with woods. Close by the church stands Kirtling Tower, an imposing, tall building which, in former times, was just the gatehouse of a mansion, Catledge Hall, demolished many years ago. Most of the moat which originally surrounded the Hall is still visible.

The Queen's Head was built in 1558, and behind a sheet of glass in the lounge is a part of the original wattle and daub construction. Brass, swords and horse brasses adorn the walls, and there is quite a collection of unusual teapots.

The food is traditional and good and you can choose, for example, from tuna and vegetable crumble, steak or chicken pies, lasagne, gammon and various curries. Should you still have room there are ice-creams or scones and coffee to follow. Flowers IPA is served, and Dry Blackthorn cider.

Children are welcome if well supervised and there is a garden for them to play in. The Queen's Head is open at lunchtime and in the evening every day and food is served throughout the week, except on Sunday evenings.

Telephone: 01638 731177

How to get there: Kirtling can be reached from the B1063, which runs between Newmarket and the A143. About ½ mile south of Newmarket town centre, take the turning for Saxon Street and Kirtling. The Queen's Head is at a road junction about 2 miles beyond Saxon Street.

Parking: There should be room in the pub's car park.

Length of the walk: 3 miles. OS map: Landranger sheet 154 Cambridge, Newmarket and surrounding area (inn GR 691571).

At first the walk is along cross-field paths to Kirtling church, passing, some way off, The Towers and skirting close to the moat with its fountains. Further on, it follows a green lane alongside Lucy Wood and continues to Stone Cottage to the west of the village. The return skirts the southern edge of Lucy Wood.

The Walk
From the Queen's Head, cross the little triangular green and, at the 'Public Footpath' sign, cross the shallow roadside ditch and take the narrow path between hedges. In about 5 yards, where the hedge on your right starts to curve left, go up a steepish bank onto a large field.

Walk across the field, aiming slightly left of straight ahead, towards a gap in the far hedge. You are walking roughly parallel with the hedge away to your left. Cross straight over a tarmac drive and continue, now with a tall hedge on the left. About 100 yards short of the field's end go left at a waymark, through a gap in the hedge. Continue amidst an uncultivated belt of shrubs for about 30 yards or so, negotiating down and up a dry, shallow ditch, and then go over a two-step stile.

Head half-right, diagonally across the field, to a wooden farm gate and go over a two-step stile close by. Join a grassy area with a moat ahead of you. See the fountain playing on your left by the farmhouse, and another round the corner to the right. Go right, pass a small white gate and go to the stile under a horse chestnut tree, taking you into the churchyard of All Saints' church.

Go left in the churchyard, which is deliberately uncultivated for wildlife to enjoy, and pass the church, with its brick chancel and interesting gargoyles. Inside are more carvings, on the roof bosses and the corbel stones. Leave the churchyard by the wicket gate, and walk out to the road.

Turn left, past the Victorian letterbox, and walk for 200 yards along the quiet footway, with big horse chestnut trees growing in the wide grass verge. Pass the Catholic church and then The Towers, and keep on until the road begins to bend to the left, by a house with lattice windows and pretty barge-boards.

Cross the road and, at the sign, enter a lane opposite the house – the green lane, not the wider track alongside it. At the end of this leafy walk go over a culvert and turn right onto a wide track, with a ditch and big trees both to left and to right.

Follow this broad track, with Lucy Wood on your left. Towards the end cross a culvert to reach a triangular clearing. Here leave the green lane, which swings half-right, and keep on a grassy path beside the wood, shortly bending a little to the left.

At the end of the wood, ignore a footbridge on the left, and keep straight on, following a hedge and ditch on the left, for another 100 yards. Here turn left, crossing the ditch by a wide culvert, and immediately turn right for a few yards, with the hedge and a deep ditch on your right.

Go half-left across the field on the marked path which leads to an internal corner, by a small wood of tall trees, known as King's Belt, where you join, obliquely, a grassy headland track which has come from the wood. The official route of the path continues in the same direction, as a headland path along the edge of the field. However, if the way ahead is obstructed, bear left on the grassy track, which shortly curves to the right to rejoin the official route by a gap in a 15 yard wide shelter belt. When partway through the shelter belt go left and over a wooden two-step stile in a fence, into a green lane. Walk for about 200 yards until you go through a wooden farm gate to a hard earth track beside Stone Cottage. Keep on beside a hedge on the left and a ranch-style fence on your right until you come out onto a road.

At this point do not join the road but turn sharp left and go

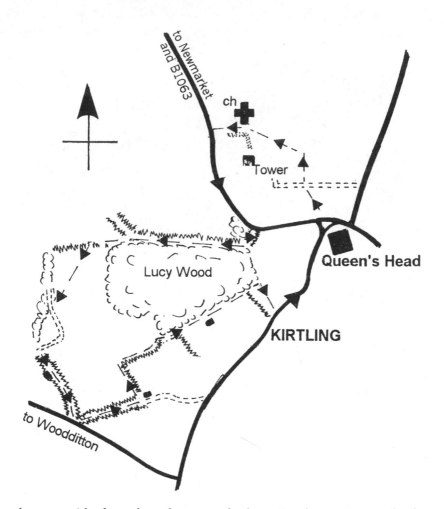

along a wide farm lane between hedges. In about 250 yards the lane becomes surfaced. Here, on the left, is a ruined brick garage, the former Primitive Methodist chapel, built in 1870.

Turn left off the lane, immediately before the chapel, and take a broad grass, headland path, with a tall hedge on the right. In 100 yards, where the hedge bends right, continue to follow the headland path until you reach the southern corner of Lucy Wood.

Turn right on a narrow footpath between the wood on the left and a ranch-type fence and in a few yards go over a stile in a

The old school house.

cross-hedge into a pasture. Keep straight on, with fenced Lucy Wood on the left. At the corner of the field go over a stile without a footpiece and continue on a narrow path between fences. There is, to the right, a small black stable building. The path leads over a stile into another field.

Keep straight on as before, following the edge of the wood. At the next corner go over two stiles in quick succession and in the following field go a further 50 yards beside the wood to a corner. Turn right and make for the right-hand corner of the field. Exit through a steel kissing-gate into a lane, which leads in a few yards to a road. Turn left along the road to the pub.

Places of interest nearby
Newmarket (in Suffolk) is only 5 miles from Kirtling. *The National Horseracing Museum*, in Newmarket High Street, is open from April till December, but not on Mondays except in the high season. Telephone: 01638 667333. *The National Stud*, on the outskirts of Newmarket, adjacent to the July Racecourse, offers guided tours (they must be booked in advance). Telephone: 01638 663464.